THE LITERARY DEVICES IN JOHN'S GOSPEL

The Johannine Monograph Series

Edited by Paul N. Anderson
and R. Alan Culpepper

The vision of The Johannine Monograph Series is to make available in printed, accessible form a selection of the most influential books on the Johannine writings in the modern era for the benefit of scholars and students alike. The volumes in this series include reprints of classic English-language texts, revised editions of significant books, and translations of important international works for English-speaking audiences. A succinct foreword by one of the editors situates each book in terms of its role within the history of Johannine scholarship, suggesting also its continuing value in the field.

This series is founded upon the conviction that scholarship is diminished when it forgets its own history and loses touch with the scintillating analyses and proposals that have shaped the course of Johannine studies. It is our hope, therefore, that the continuing availability of these important works will help to keep the cutting-edge scholarship of this and coming generations of scholars engaged with the classic works of Johannine scholarship while they also chart new directions for the future of the discipline.

THE LITERARY DEVICES
IN JOHN'S GOSPEL

REVISED AND EXPANDED EDITION

by
DAVID W. WEAD

Edited by
PAUL N. ANDERSON and R. ALAN CULPEPPER

Foreword by
R. ALAN CULPEPPER

WIPF & STOCK · Eugene, Oregon

THE LITERARY DEVICES IN JOHN'S GOSPEL
Revised and Expanded Edition

Johannine Monograph Series 6

Wipf & Stock
An Imprint of Wipf and Stock Publishers
199 W. 8th Ave., Suite 3
Eugene, OR 97401

www.wipfandstock.com

PAPERBACK ISBN: 978-1-5326-4720-8
HARDCOVER ISBN: 978-1-5326-4721-5
EBOOK ISBN: 978-1-5326-4722-2

Manufactured in the U.S.A.   10/10/18

CONTENTS

ABBREVIATIONS

AB	Anchor Bible
Bib	*Biblica*
BINS	Bible Interpretation Series
BZ	*Biblische Zeitschrift*
CBC	Cambridge Bible Commentary
ConBNT	Coniectanea Neotestamentica or Coniectanea Biblica: New Testament Series
ETL	*Ephemerides Theologicae Lovanienses*
ExpT	*Expository Times*
HBS	Herders Biblische Studien
HNT	Handbuch zum Neuen Testament
HThKNT	Herders Theologischer Kommentar zum Neuen Testament
HUCA	*Hebrew Union College Annual*
ICC	International Critical Commentary
Int	*Interpretation*
JTS	*Journal of Theological Studies*
JSNTSS	Journal for the Study of the New Testament Supplement Series
KEK	Kritisch-exegetischer Kommentar über das Neue Testament
LCL	Loeb Classical Library
LNTS	Library of New Testament Studies
NovTSup	Supplements to Novum Testamentum
NTD	Das Neue Testament Deutsch

NTS	*New Testament Studies*
RGG3	*Religion in Geschichte und Gegenwart.* 3rd ed. Edited by Kurt Galling and Wilfred Werbeck. Tübingen: Mohr Siebeck, 1965
RHPR	*Revue d'histoire et de philosophie religeuses*
RSPT	*Revue des sciences philosophiques et théologiques*
RSR	*Recherches de science religieuse*
RTP	*Revue de théologie et de philosophie*
SBLMS	Society of Biblical Literature Monograph Series
SBS	Stuttgarter Bibelstudien
SBT	Studies in Biblical Theology
SE	*Studia Evangelica*
SJ	Studia Judaica
SNTSMS	Society for New Testament Studies Monograph Series
SPAW	*Sitzungsberichte der preussischen Akademie der Wissenschaften*
SSN	Studia Semitica Neerlandica
ST	*Studia Theologica*
SympS	Symposium Series
TBT	Theologische Bibliothek Töpelmann
TLZ	*Theologische Literaturezeitung*
TNTC	Tyndale New Testament Commentaries
TU	Texte und Untersuchungen
TWNT	*Theologische Wörterbuch zum Neuen Testament.*
TZ	*Theologische Zeitschrift*
WUNT	*Wissenschaftliche Untersuchungen zum Neuen Testament*
ZNW	*Zeitschrift für die neutestamentliche Wissenschaft*

DAVID W. WEAD'S CONTRIBUTION
TO JOHANNINE SCHOLARSHIP

BY R. ALAN CULPEPPER

Sometimes a small volume anticipates perspectives that become widely accepted only in coming decades. One thinks of Martin Kähler, *Der soge-nannte historische Jesus und der geschichtliche, biblische Christus*, published in 1892 (109 pages in the English translation),[1] and Percival Gardner-Smith, *Saint John and the Synoptic Gospels*, 1938 (one hundred pages).[2] David W. Wead's *The Literary Devices in John's Gospel*, originally published in 1970 (114 pages), is such a volume.

It was written as a dissertation in Basel between 1966 and 1968 under the supervision of Bo Reicke, with Oscar Cullmann serving as the second reader. In order to appreciate the significance of this volume, one must revisit Johannine scholarship in the late sixties, which (on the continent) was fully engaged in dialogue with Rudolf Bultmann.[3] Gospel scholarship in general was dominated by historical criticism and was still appropriating redaction criticism.

In this context, Wead's dissertation had little immediate impact, and was even greeted with suspicion. *New Testament Abstracts* carried a synopsis of the review by K. M. Fischer in *Theologische Literatur Zeitschrift* 97.3 (1972) 192–94, which concluded, "In general, the author has defined his task so narrowly that he avoids the major problems connected with Jn. Although he never makes his conservative viewpoint explicit, it can be perceived easily." In effect, understanding the ways the evangelist communicated the gospel's message through its literary devices is not as important as the questions regarding its authorship, sources, setting, and issues of

1. Kähler, *So-Called Historical Jesus*.

2. Gardner-Smith, *Saint John*.

3. See the forewords in the re-publications of Bultmann, *Gospel of John*, written by Paul N. Anderson; and Smith, *Composition and Order*, written by R. Alan Culpepper.

history and theology.[4] Furthermore, the reviewer implies that addressing the role of the literary devices in John, rather than historical-critical issues, is motivated at least in part by the author's "conservative viewpoint."

Wead's work has also been largely overlooked in reviews of the development of Johannine scholarship and narrative criticism. Robert Kysar's review of Johannine scholarship during the decade of 1963–73 does not cite Wead, and contains no discussion of John as literature or John's literary devices.[5] Hartwig Thyen's extensive review of literature on the Gospel of John in *Theologische Rundschau* lists Wead's dissertation, but does not comment on it.[6] Neither does Norman R. Petersen take note of Wead's *Literary Devices* in his Guides to Biblical Scholarship volume on *Literary Criticism for New Testament Critics* in 1978,[7] nor does Mark Allan Powell cite Wead in *What Is Narrative Criticism?* (1990).[8] In Stephen D. Moore's 1989 review and analysis of the emergence of literary criticism of the gospels, Wead's volume is listed in the bibliography, but not discussed.[9] It is only in Tom Thatcher's review of the development of narrative criticism in *Anatomies of Criticism* that its significance is adequately noted:

> David Wead's *The Literary Devices in John's Gospel* . . . was the first sustained attempt to analyze the narrative dynamics of the Fourth Gospel using models adapted from secular literary theory. . . . the main topics of his analysis have featured largely in almost all subsequent discussion of the Fourth Gospel as narrative: point of view, double entendre, irony, and metaphor.[10]

A quick review of the introductions to the three leading commentaries on John published in the fifties and sixties—C. K. Barrett (1955), Raymond E. Brown (1966–1970), and Rudolf Schnackenburg, vol 1 (1965, English translation in 1968)—is similarly revealing. Neither Barrett nor Schnackenburg contain any discussion of John's literary devices. The first section of Barrett's 121-page introduction is entitled "The Gospel, its Characteristics and

---

4. *New Testament Abstracts* 17.1 (1972) 176r, synopsis of the review by K. M. Fischer in *Theologische Literatur Zeitschrift* 97.3 (1972) 192–94; see also the review by Smith ("Book Review," 119–20).

5. Kysar, *Fourth Evangelist and His Gospel*.

6. Thyen, "Aus der Literatur," 43.

7. Peterson, *Literary Criticism*.

8. Powell, *What Is Narrative Criticism?*

9. Moore, *Literary Criticism and the Gospels*.

10. Thatcher and Moore, *Anatomies of Narrative Criticism*, 12.

Purpose," but the subsection on "Literary Characteristics and Structure" discusses the gospel's vocabulary and evidence of Aramaic influence on John's Greek.[11] The third section of Schnackenburg's 217-page introduction is entitled "Literary Criticism of the Gospel of St. John," but it deals with the issues of literary unity, sources, displacement, and redaction. Following a brief discussion of John 4:44 as a redactional note, Schnackenburg adds, "there are perhaps other brief comments which are to be attributed to the editors."[12] The 146-page introduction in Raymond Brown's Anchor Bible commentary, which devotes a page and a half to "Notable Characteristics in Johannine Style," contains a paragraph on each of the following: (1) inclusion, (2) chiasm, (3) twofold or double meaning, (4) misunderstanding, (5) irony, and (6) explanatory notes.[13] Brown's bibliography for this section lists five sources: Clavier on irony, Cullmann on double meaning, Léon-Dufour and Lund on chiasm, and Tenney on explanatory notes.[14] This survey of the three leading commentaries published in the fifties and sixties shows that, at the time Wead wrote his dissertation, historical-critical concerns with the backgrounds, authorship, setting, sources, and literary unity of the gospel were so dominant that its literary devices and narrative character scarcely registered on the commentators' radars.[15]

As a further diagnostic of the state of literary theory in the sixties and the orientation of Wead's work, one can survey works on literary theory published prior to 1967. In the following sample, Wead interacts with those titles marked with an asterisk:

Auerbach, Erich. *Mimesis: The Representation of Reality in Western Literature.* Translated by W. R. Trask. Princeton, NJ: Princeton University Press, 1953.
Booth, Wayne C. "Distance and Point of View: An Essay in Classification." *Essays in Criticism* 11 (1961) 60–79.
*———. *The Rhetoric of Fiction.* Chicago: Chicago University Press, 1961.
Brooks, Cleanth, and Robert Penn Warren. *Understanding Fiction.* New York: Crofts, 1943.
Forster, E. M. *Aspects of the Novel.* New York: Penguin, 1962.

11. Barrett, *Gospel*, 5–11.

12. Schnackenburg, *Gospel*, 58.

13. Brown, *Gospel According to John (i–xii)*, cxxxv–cxxxvi.

14. Henri Clavier, "L'Ironie," 261–76; Oscar Cullmann, "Johanneische Gebrauch," 360–72; Léon-Dufour, "Trois Chiasmes Johanniques," 249–55; Lund, "Influence of Chiasmus," 27–48, 405–33; Tenney, "Footnotes of John's Gospel," 350–64.

15. See further regarding C. H. Dodd my essay, "C. H. Dodd as a Precursor," 31–48; and van der Watt's essay, "Symbolism in John's Gospel," 66–85.

*Frye, Northrop. *Anatomy of Criticism: Four Essays.* Princeton, NJ: Princeton University Press, 1957.

Harris, Wendell V. "Mapping Fiction's Forest of Symbols." In *University of Colorado Studies,* 133–46. Studies in Language and Literature 9. Boulder: University of Colorado Press, 1963.

Harvey, W. J. *Character and the Novel.* London: Chatto & Windus, 1965.

Hirsch, E. D., Jr. *Validity in Interpretation.* New Haven: Yale University Press, 1967.

Ingarden, Roman. *Das Literarische Kunstwerk.* Tübingen, Germany: Niemeyer, 1960.

*Jónsson, Jakob. *Humor and Irony in the New Testament.* Reykjavik, Iceland: Menningarsjóts, 1965.

Kermode, Frank. *The Sense of an Ending: Studies in the Theory of Fiction.* London: Oxford University Press, 1967.

Krieger, Murray. *A Window to Criticism: Shakespeare's Sonnets and Modern Poetics.* Princeton, NJ: Princeton University Press, 1964.

Langer, Susanne K. *Philosophy in a New Key: A Study in the Symbolism of Reason, Rite, and Art.* 4th ed. Cambridge: Harvard University Press, 1960.

Lemon, Lee T., and Marion J. Reis, eds. and trans. *Russian Formalist Criticism.* Lincoln: University of Nebraska Press, 1965.

Levin, Harry. *Contexts of Criticism.* Harvard Studies in Comparative Literature 22. Cambridge: Harvard University Press, 1957.

*Lubbock, Percy. *The Craft of Fiction.* The Travellers' Library. London: Cape, 1921.

Sacks, Sheldon. *Fiction and the Shape of Belief: A Study of Henry Fielding, with Glances at Swift, Johnson, and Richardson.* Berkeley: University of California Press, 1964.

Scholes, Robert, ed. *Approaches to the Novel: Materials for a Poetics.* Rev. ed. San Francisco: Chandler, 1966.

Scholes, Robert, and Robert Kellogg. *The Nature of Narrative.* London: Oxford University Press, 1966.

Sontag, Susan. *Against Interpretation and Other Essays.* New York: Noonday, 1966.

Stevick, Philip, ed. *The Theory of the Novel.* New York: Free, 1967.

*Thompson, A. R. *The Dry Mock: A Study of Irony in Drama.* Berkeley: University of California Press, 1948.

*Thomson, J. A. K. *Irony: An Historical Investigation.* London: Allen & Unwin, 1926.

Wheelwright, Philip E. *Metaphor and Reality.* Bloomington: Indiana University Press, 1962.

This diagnostic sample illuminates the chronological, geographical, and critical setting of *Literary Devices*. Noticeably absent is the work in English and American literary theory, which is understandable in a dissertation written in Basel, the mirror image of the neglect of continental scholarship in many American dissertations. This sample also reflects the setting of Wead's work, continuing dominance of historical criticism, and the lack of engagement with literary theory arising from scholarship on works of fiction.

What one finds instead is that Wead grounded his analysis of John's literary devices in ancient literary theory, regularly drawing on references in

Homer, Plato, Aristotle, and Sophocles, in particular, and also Hermogenes of Tarsus. He also interacts with an impressive range of continental scholars in the fields of the New Testament, Classics, and Literary Theory whose work is little noticed today. For example, in the discussion of metaphor in chapter 5 one finds references to Jülicher (1910), Konrad (1939), Stählin (1913), Stanford (1936), and Stern (1931), among others.[16] A quick glance at the bibliography of this book will reveal many other older sources and German scholars whose work is seldom consulted today. *Literary Devices* can therefore serve as a valuable guide to this literature.

Whereas Wead draws heavily from continental, especially German New Testament scholarship, a decade later narrative criticism arose through engagement with American, Czech, English, French, Israeli, and Russian literary theory.[17] Note the nationalities of the authors and the diverse varieties of literary theories represented in the following sample of titles from 1968–1980:

Booth, Wayne C. *A Rhetoric of Irony.* Chicago: University of Chicago Press, 1974.
Casparis, Christian P. *Tense without Time: The Present Tense in Narration.* Swiss Studies in English 84. Bern, Switzerland: Verlag, 1975.
Chambers, Ross. "Commentary in Literary Texts." *Critical Inquiry* 5 (1978) 323–37.
Chatman, Seymour. *Story and Discourse: Narrative Structure in Fiction and Film.* Ithaca. NY: Cornell University Press, 1978.
Cohen, Ted. "Metaphor and the Cultivation of Intimacy." *Critical Inquiry* 5 (1978) 3–12.
Eco, Umberto. *The Role of the Reader: Explorations in the Semiotics of Texts.* Bloomington: Indiana University Press, 1979.
Egan, Kieran. "What is a Plot?" *New Literary History* 9 (1978) 455–73.
Fawcett, Thomas. *The Symbolic Language of Religion: An Introductory Study.* London: SCM, 1970.
Fish, Stanley E. *Is There a Text in This Class? The Authority of Interpretive Communities.* Cambridge: Harvard University Press, 1980.
Freedman, William. "The Literary Motif: A Definition and Evaluation." *Novel* 4 (1971) 123–31.
Friedman, Norman. *Form and Meaning in Fiction.* Athens, Georgia: University of Georgia Press, 1975.
Frye, Northrop. "The Critical Path: An Essay on the Social Context of Literary Criticism." In *In Search of Literary Theory*, edited by M. W. Bloomfield, 91–104. Ithaca, NY: Cornell University Press, 1972.

16. Jülicher, *Die Gleichnisreden Jesu*; Konrad, *Ètude sur la Métaphore*; Stählin, *Zur Psychologie*; Stanford, *Greek Metaphor*; Stern, *Meaning and Change of Meaning.*

17. See the fine discussions in Petersen, *Literary Criticism*, 9–23; Peterson, "Literary Criticism in Biblical Studies," 25–50; and Moore, *Literary Criticism*, especially the sections "Immigrant Concepts in Narrative Criticism" (7–13) and "Point of View in Mark" (26–28).

Genette, Gérard. *Narrative Discourse: An Essay in Method*. Translated by Jane E. Lewin. Ithaca: Cornell University Press, 1980.

Gunn, Giles. *The Interpretation of Otherness: Literature, Religion, and the American Imagination*. London: Oxford University Press, 1979.

Ingarden, Roman. *The Cognition of the Literary Work of Art*. Translated by R. A. Crowley and K. R. Olson. Evanston, IL: Northwestern University Press, 1973.

Iser, Wolfgang. *The Act of Reading: A Theory of Aesthetic Response*. Baltimore: Johns Hopkins University Press, 1978.

————. *The Implied Reader: Patterns of Communication in Prose Fiction from Bunyan to Beckett*. Baltimore: Johns Hopkins University Press, 1974.

Kermode, Frank. "Figures in the Carpet: On Recent Theories of Narrative Discourse." In *Comparative Criticism, A Yearbook: 2*, edited by Elinor S. Shaffer, 291–301. Cambridge: Cambridge University Press, 1980.

————. *Genesis of Secrecy: On the Interpretation of Narrative*. The Charles Eliot Norton Lectures. Cambridge: Harvard University Press, 1979.

Lakoff, George, and Mark Johnson. *Metaphors We Live By*. Chicago: University of Chicago Press, 1980.

Lotman, J. M. "Point of View in a Text." *New Literary History* 6 (1975) 339–52.

Mailloux, Steven. "Reader-Response Criticism?" *Genre* 10 (1977) 413–31.

Muecke, D. C. *The Compass of Irony*. London: Methuen, 1969.

————. *Irony*. The Critical Idiom 13. London: Methuen, 1970.

Ong, Walter J. *Interfaces of the Word: Studies in the Evolution of Consciousness and Culture*. Ithaca, NY: Cornell University Press, 1977.

Piwowarczyk, Mary Ann. "The Narratee and the Situation of Enunciation: A Reconsideration of Prince's Theory." *Genre* 9 (1976) 161–77.

Prince, Gerald. "Introduction à l'Étude du Narrataire." *Poetique* 14 (1973) 178–96.

————. "Notes Toward a Categorization of Fictional 'Narratees.'" *Genre* 4 (1971) 100–105.

————. "On Readers and Listeners in Narrative." *Neophilologus* 55 (1971) 117–22.

Rabinowitz, Peter J. "Truth in Fiction: A Reexamination of Audiences." *Critical Inquiry* 4 (1977) 121–41.

Ricoeur, Paul. *Interpretation Theory: Discourse and the Surplus of Meaning*. Fort Worth: Texas Christian University Press, 1976.

————. "Narrative Time." *Critical Inquiry* 7 (1980) 169–90.

Russell, D. A., and M. Winterbottom, eds. *Ancient Literary Criticism: The Principal Texts in New Translations*. Oxford: Clarendon, 1972.

Smith, Jonathan Z. "The Influence of Symbols upon Social Change: A Place on Which to Stand." *Worship* 44 (1970) 457–74.

Sternberg, Meir. *Expositional Modes and Temporal Ordering in Fiction*. Baltimore: Johns Hopkins University Press, 1978.

Tompkins, Jane P., ed. *Reader-Response Criticism: From Formalism to Post-Structuralism*. Baltimore: Johns Hopkins University Press, 1980.

Uspensky, Boris. *A Poetics of Composition: The Structure of the Artistic Text and Typology of a Compositional Form*. Translated by V. Zavarin and S. Wittig. Berkeley: University of California Press, 1973.

White, Hayden. "The Value of Narrativity in the Representation of Reality." *Critical Inquiry* 7 (1980) 5–27.

Wicker, Brian. *The Story-Shaped World: Fiction and Metaphysics, Some Variations on a Theme*. Notre Dame: University of Notre Dame Press, 1975.

Wilson, Rawdon. "The Bright Chimera: Character as a Literary Term." *Critical Inquiry* 5 (1979) 725–49.

Wittig, Susan. "A Theory of Multiple Meanings." *Semeia* 9 (1977) 75–103.

Wolff, Erwin. "Der Intendierte Leser." *Poetica* 4 (1971) 141–66.

At the same time, New Testament scholars began to turn their attention to the literary aspects of the Gospels and read the current work on literary criticism:

Beardslee, William A. *Literary Criticism of the New Testament.* Guides to Biblical Scholarship. Philadelphia: Fortress, 1970.

Brewer, Derek. "The Gospels and the Laws of Folktale: A Centenary Lecture, 14 June 1978." *Folklore* 90 (1979) 37–52.

Caird, G. B. *The Language and Imagery of the Bible.* London: Duckworth, 1980.

Collins, Raymond F. "The Representative Figures of the Fourth Gospel—I." *Downside Review* 94 (1976) 26–46.

———. "The Representative Figures of the Fourth Gospel—II." *Downside Review* 95 (1976) 118–32.

Crossan, John Dominic. "Literary Criticism and Biblical Hermeneutics." *Journal of Religion* 57 (1977) 76–80.

Dewey, Kim. "*Paroimiai* in the Gospel of John." *Semeia* 17 (1980) 81–100.

Frei, Hans. *The Eclipse of Biblical Narrative: A Study in Eighteenth and Nineteenth Century Hermeneutics.* New Haven: Yale University Press, 1974.

Hawkin, David J. "The Function of the Beloved Disciple Motif in the Johannine Redaction." *Laval Theologique et Philosophique* 33 (1977) 135–50.

Leroy, Herbert. *Rätsel und Missverständnis: Ein Beitrag zur Formgeschichte des Johannesevangeliums.* Bonner Biblische Beiträge 30. Bonn: Hanstein, 1968.

MacRae, George W. "Theology and Irony in the Fourth Gospel." In *The Word in the World: Essays in Honor of Frederick L. Moriarity, S. J.*, edited by R. J. Clifford, S. J., and G. W. MacRae, S. J., 83–96. Cambridge: Weston College Press, 1973.

Nuttall, Geoffrey. *The Moment of Recognition: Luke as Story-Teller.* Ethel M. Wood Lecture 1978. London: Athlone Press, 1978.

Olsson, Birger. *Structure and Meaning in the Fourth Gospel: A Text-Linguistic Analysis of John 2:1–11 and 4:1–42.* Translated by J. Gray. Coniectanea Biblica: New Testament 6. Lund, Sweden: Gleerup, 1974.

O'Rourke, John J. "Asides in the Gospel of John." *Novum Testamentum* 21 (1979) 210–19.

———. "The Historic Present in the Gospel of John." *Journal of Biblical Literature* 93 (1974) 585–90.

Painter, John. "Johannine Symbols: A Case Study in Epistemology." *Journal of Theology for Southern Africa* 27 (1979) 26–41.

Petersen, Norman R. *Literary Criticism for New Testament Critics.* Guides to Biblical Scholarship. Philadelphia: Fortress, 1978.

———. "'Point of View' in Mark's Narrative." *Semeia* 12 (1978) 97–121.

———. "When is the End not the End? Literary Reflections on the Ending of Mark's Narrative." *Interpretation* 34 (1980) 151–66.

Ryken, Leland. "Literary Criticism and the Bible: Some Fallacies." In *Literary Interpretations of Biblical Narratives*, edited by K. R. R. Gros Louis et al., 24–40. Nashville: Abingdon, 1974.

Schneiders, Sandra M. "History and Symbolism in the Fourth Gospel." In *L'Evangile de Jean: Sources, Redaction, Théologie*, edited by Marinus de Jonge, 371–76. Bibliotheca Ephemeridum Theologicarum Lovaniensium 44. Gembloux, Belgium: Duculot, 1977.

———. "Symbolism and the Sacramental Principle in the Fourth Gospel." In *Segni e sacramenti nel Vangelo di Giovanni*, edited by Pius-Ramon Tragan, 221–35. Studia Anselmiana 66. Rome: Anselmiana, 1977.

Spencer, Richard A., ed. *Orientation by Disorientation: Studies in Literary Criticism, Presented in Honor of William A. Beardslee*. Pittsburgh Theological Monograph Series 35. Pittsburgh: Pickwick, 1980.

Stemberger, Günter. *La Symbolique du Bien et du Mal selon Saint Jean*. Parole de Dieu. Paris: Seuil, 1970.

Tannehill, Robert C. "Tension in Synoptic Sayings and Stories." *Interpretation* 34 (1980) 138–50.

Tenney, M. C. "The Footnotes of John's Gospel." *Bibliotheca Sacra* (1960) 350–64.

Wead, David W. "The Johannine Double Meaning." *Restoration Quarterly* 13 (1970) 106–20.

———. "Johannine Irony as a Key to the Author-Audience Relationship in John's Gospel." In *AAR Biblical Literature: 1974*, compiled by Fred O. Francis, 33–50. Missoula, MT: Scholars, 1974.

———. *The Literary Devices in John's Gospel*. Theologischen Dissertationen 4. Basel, Switzerland: Reinhart, 1970.

Wilder, Amos N. *Early Christian Rhetoric: The Language of the Gospel*. Cambridge: Harvard University Press, 1971.

The challenges to historical criticism and the appetite for new approaches to interpretation were so sharp by 1980 that Leander E. Keck felt the need to write an essay entitled "Will the Historical-Critical Method Survive? Some Observations."[18]

With this historical context in mind, we may now turn to the pioneering journey Wead makes in *Literary Devices in John's Gospel*. As he grapples for an appropriate title for his work, Wead eschews the debate about hermeneutics, with its tilt toward "the ontology of the individuals" involved in the interpretive process—an oblique reference to demythologizing and "the new hermeneutics."[19] Instead, he retains the emphasis on the author rather than the interpreter. John's literary devices "become the modes of thought in which he [the author] wished to convey his message." Nevertheless, these

18. Keck, "Historical-Critical Method," 115–27.

19. See, for example, William G. Doty's discussion of "the new hermeneutic" in *Contemporary New Testament Interpretation*, 28–43.

devices "are vehicles of thought that must be recognized and interpreted" (33).[20]

1. POST-RESURRECTION POINT OF VIEW

Following the lead of Henry James and Percy Lubbock, Wead first takes up the role of point of view, and especially the evangelist's post-resurrection point of view. He asks the three questions posed by Francis X. Connolly: (1) Who is telling the story? (2) From what physical point of view? And (3) from what mode or mental point of view? Wead identifies the storyteller in the Gospel of John as the Beloved Disciple, who from a post-resurrection perspective reports not only what happened, but its significance as it came to be understood in light of the resurrection. The "omniscient author" can also speak of the role of the Logos from "the beginning" and provide commentary on Palestinian customs, the disciples' lack of understanding, and information about the characters. In a footnote (7 n. 16), Wead acknowledges the danger of anachronism in finding modern literary techniques in the work of an ancient author, and in doing so he identifies a criticism that would be leveled against narrative criticism:

> It must be remembered that John is not a modern author. For this reason, we have limited ourselves from many of the modern nuances and discussions concerning the point of view. That which is the modern writer's prerogative was not understood or intended by the ancient author.[21]

The matter of authorial intent, as well as a recognition of the importance of narrative rhetoric, emerges again when Wead comments, "The crucial question becomes for us not 'What did Nicodemus understand?' but 'What is John wishing his readers to understand?'" (10). Here again is a move away from concern with historicity toward rhetoric, but one that is not explored further.

As a matter of coherence, Wead finds that, in John's Gospel, "the mental point of view that is coherent with the physical point of view. The physical to a large extent determines the mental, but both are coherent with one another and complement one another." (11) That is, the evangelist's

20. References to *Literary Devices in John's Gospel* are placed in the text in parentheses.

21. See the similar comment in Culpepper, *Anatomy of the Fourth Gospel*, 8–9; and examples of this critique in Carson, *Gospel*, 39–40, 63–68; and de Boer, "Narrative Criticism," 35–48.

theological perspective on the resurrection, the Holy Spirit, and the fulfillment of the scriptures, for example, is coherent with his post-resurrection
point of view. This coherence with respect to point of view, Wead affirms,
supports the grammatical analyses of Eduard Schweizer, Eugen Ruckstuhl,
and Bent Noack as it "speaks for the unitive composition of the Gospel"
(11).[22] The Fourth Evangelist may have drawn on sources and the tradition of a community, but he wrote as an eyewitness who was guided by the
Holy Spirit. This post-resurrection point of view is foundational because it
becomes the basis for the rest of the Gospel's literary devices.

Literary analysis of point of view in narratives was greatly advanced
by the work of Boris Uspensky in 1973.[23] Uspensky defined fives aspects or
"planes" of point of view: the ideological (evaluative norms), the phraseo-
logical (speech patterns), the spatial (location of the narrator), the temporal
(the time of the narrator), and the psychological (internal and external to
the characters).[24] Seymour Chatman (1978) distinguished the real author,
the implied author, and the narrator and discussed point of view and its
relation to narrative voice.[25] Gérard Genette (1980) distinguished the questions of "who sees?" and "who speaks?" (mood and voice). The narrator
may be a character in the story or not, and the narrator may provide internal analysis of events or outside observation of events. The former bears on
the identity of the narrator, while the latter on the narrator's point of view.[26]

Wead's chapter on point of view in the Gospel of John stands at the
head of what has become a rich, ongoing discussion of this aspect of the
gospel narrative. As Tom Thatcher noted (see footnote 10 of this foreword),
virtually every narrative-critical work on John has followed Wead's lead in
discussing point of view and the other literary devices he identified in the
Gospel.[27]

22. Schweizer, *Ego Eimi*; Ruckstuhl, *Die literarische Einheit*; Noack, *Zur Johanneisch-
en Tradition*.

23. Uspensky, *Poetics of Composition*.

24. Uspensky, *Poetics of Composition*, 6, and passim.

25. Chatman, *Story and Discourse*, 146–58.

26. Genette, *Narrative Discourse*, 186.

27. See Culpepper, *Anatomy of the Fourth Gospel*, 15–49; Belle, *Les Parentheses*;
Staley, *Print's First Kiss*; Resseguie, *Strange Gospel*.

2. THE JOHANNINE SIGN

Wead treats the Johannine *semeia* as literary devices, arguing that their primary background is the Old Testament, where signs may serve as warnings or confirm the revelation brought by Moses and the prophets. This authenticating function is particularly significant for John. Contrary to the pattern of omens in classical Greek literature, "To the Hebrew mind, the word of God came first, and then the sign was given to authenticate the word" (19). For John, the emphasis is not on Jesus' miracles, but on their meaning. Wead identifies seven signs in John: three pairs (John 2 and 4, 5 and 6, 9 and 11) and the resurrection. The latter differs from the other six in that the event itself is not narrated, but four events in John 20 and 21 following the resurrection clarify its meaning.

When he turns to the theological implications of the signs and their interpretation in John, Wead raises the question of whether the symbolic significance of the signs casts doubt on their historicity, and the issue of historicity seems to take precedence over further exploration of the literary functions of the Johannine signs. Wead's response is that "we have no precedent that such events ever existed in purely symbolic form, or that through the quest for a symbolic meaning historical events were created" (30). The witness function of the signs is also essential for John: "Signs must be interpreted as actions meant to call persons to faith and to reveal the nature of the Messiah" (31). Closely related in Jewish literature is the eschatological significance of the signs as they point to the messianic age and confirm the arrival of the Messiah. In John, the signs establish Jesus' messianic authority, but the announcement of the messianic salvation is not limited to the signs and the discourses related to them.

Wead laments the "fuzziness" of the term "symbolic" and calls for more attention to the symbolic significance of the signs, but urges caution in the interpretation of symbolism in John, claiming, "we have no precedent in this genre of literature for the hidden symbolic interpretation of a text" (33). The pattern seems to be that John accords symbolic significance to the signs, but we cannot assume that the signs are symbolic actions; when that is the case, John signals this interpretive significance to the reader (34). Above all, following the Old Testament pattern, the sign authenticates the word of the prophet.

Perhaps surprisingly, narrative-critical scholarship has not followed Wead's lead in analyzing the role of the signs in John as a discrete topic.[28] On the other hand, debate over the existence and content of a signs source has continued unabated.[29] Similarly, John's symbolism has attracted a great deal of attention.[30] I treated symbolism as an aspect of implicit commentary.[31] Dorothy A. Lee studied the symbolic narratives in John,[32] and Craig R. Koester addressed the topic from both literary and historical perspectives.[33] Several individual symbols have attracted analysis, especially water symbolism,[34] temple symbolism,[35] the imagery in John 10 and 15,[36] and the symbolism related to Jesus' death.[37] Ruben Zimmermann and Paul N. Anderson have proposed ways of systematizing the range of symbols in John.[38]

3. THE JOHANNINE DOUBLE MEANING

As a literary device, Wead finds double meaning in those instances where "the author uses words with two meanings, both of which may be applicable" and where the author "employs a distinctive device, where both

---

28. See, however, my essay "Cognition in John," 251–60.

29. See, for example, Smith, *Composition and Order*; Fortna, *Gospel of Signs*; Fortna, *Fourth Gospel*; Belle, *Signs Source*; Von Wahlde, *Gospel and Letters of John*.

30. Günter Stemberger, *La Symbolique*; Schneiders, "History and Symbolism," 371–76; Schneiders, "Symbolism," 221–35; Painter, "Johannine Symbols," 26–41; Léon-Dufour, "Towards a Symbolic Reading," 439–56; Paschal, "Sacramental Symbolism and Physical Imagery in the Gospel of John," 151–76; Akala, *Son-Father Relationship*.

31. Culpepper, *Anatomy of the Fourth Gospel*, 180–98.

32. Lee, *Symbolic Narratives*.

33. Koester, *Symbolism in the Fourth Gospel*.

34. Jones, *Symbol of Water*; Ng, *Water Symbolism in John*.

35. Coloe, *God Dwells with Us*; Coloe, *Dwelling*; Busse, *Das Johannesevanglium*, esp. 323–402; Kerr, *Temple of Jesus' Body*; Schneiders, "Raising of the New Temple," 337–55; Um, *Theme of Temple Christology*; Chanikuzhy, *Jesus, the Eschatological Temple*.

36. Note: imagery and symbolism are closely related, so the two are being treated together here for convenience. See van der Watt, "Interpreting Imagery," 272–82; van der Watt, "Ethics Alive in Imagery," 421–48.

37. Zumstein, "Johannes 19, 25–27," 156–77; Culpepper, "Symbolism and History," 39–54.

38. Zimmermann, *Christologie der Bilder*; Zimmermann, "Opening Up Paths," 1–43; Anderson, "Gradations of Symbolization," 157–94.

meanings of the word apply" (37).[39] Examining this device in John, Wead identifies six ways in which double meaning is conveyed:

> (1) the double meanings based on the Greek alone; (2) the double meanings based on both the Greek and the Aramaic, or Hebrew terminology behind it; (3) the possible double meaning that is derived from an Aramaic double meaning which does not come into the Greek text; (4) the double meaning of words used in a pericope or parable-like saying; (5) the double meaning of verbs based on the ambiguity of mode; and (6) the words which rely on a figurative meaning for the fuller expression of the meaning of the evangelist. (38)

The use of the word ἄνωθεν in John 3:3 is a prime example of the first category; the word has two meanings ("again"/"from above"), both of which may be intended. Following this definition of double meaning, Wead does not find double meaning in the other occurrences of this term in the Gospel, where it may have a figurative or symbolic sense as well as its literal meaning.[40] Wead's discussion of John's use of ὕψοω as an example of the second category (though he notes that understanding of the meaning of the Hebrew is not required (42) leads him into an extended discussion of the interpretation of Jesus' crucifixion in John (43–45). John's concept of the "Lamb of God" is cited as an example of the third category—double meaning derived from an Aramaic double meaning that does not come into the text of the Gospel (47).[41] The double meaning of πνεῦμα ("wind"/"spirit") serves as an example of the fourth category, where the double meaning of a word is developed in a short pericope or parable-like saying, as in Jesus' dialogue with Nicodemus in John 3. Wead describes the dynamics as follows:

> Thus, again we find a word picture and its meaning so closely united that they cannot be separated, even as they are described

39. Here Wead followed the lead of one of his professors, since Oscar Cullmann had explored this topic earlier in "Der Johanneische," 360–72.

40. See my suggestion that ἄνωθεν has a second nuance when it is used John 19:11, regarding Pilate's authority (to convict Jesus) "from above" (the Roman emperor/God) and in 19:23, regarding the seamless tunic woven "from above" (from the top down/ by God, if the tunic is another of John's images related to the unity God intends for the church). See Culpepper, "Theology," 21–37; Culpepper, "Designs for the Church," 376–92; Culpepper, "Symbolism and History," 39–54.

41. In his review in *Theologische Literatur Zeitschrift* 97.3 (1972) 192–94, K. M. Fischer questioned the legitimacy of this category, given Wead's admission that the double meaning does not appear in the Gospel.

> with the same words. The unseen action of the wind expresses the
> unknowable actions of the Spirit. The figure is not described with
> symbolic language, nor is the application. Both come from the
> actual meanings of the words. (51)

The double meaning present in the Greek text simply cannot be conveyed in an English translation. The fifth category, "ambiguity found in various verb forms, particularly the second person plural, may be indicative or imperative," was discussed by F. W. Gingrich.[42] Words that rely on figurative meaning for the author's full expression, the sixth category, include νὺξ (9:4, literal or figurative night) and κοιμάω (11:11–14, "sleep"/"die"). The recurrence of double meanings shows that this is a common literary device in John but, Wead insists, it cannot be assumed in every instance of a given word; each occurrence must be assessed.

Wead himself subsequently published an article on double meaning in John.[43] While this topic is perhaps overdue for a fresh treatment, it has generally been absorbed into the studies listed here regarding imagery, symbolism, misunderstanding, and irony. See, for example, Gail R. O'Day's contention that both levels of meaning (the literal and the ironic) are intended in John's irony.[44]

4. IRONY IN THE FOURTH GOSPEL

Wead's analysis of Johannine irony is grounded in the modes of irony Bishop Thirwall identified in Sophocles and the ancient Greek tragedians (59).[45] Wead defines irony broadly as "a statement (usually an understatement) or an action by which the author or character intends to convey another meaning than that which the words superficially carry" (62). This disparity of meaning is created by the author, who provides the reader with information and an understanding of the entire context of the action that the characters do not have. John's irony, therefore, grows naturally out of the author's post-resurrection point of view. In ancient drama, the audience knew the plot—the events were well-known, and prologues were used to assure this knowledge. The audience looked for how the dramatist would

42. Gingrich, "Ambiguity," 77.

43. Wead, "Johannine Double Meaning," 106–20. See also Richard, "Expressions of Double Meaning," 96–112.

44. O'Day, *Revelation in the Fourth Gospel*, 24.

45. Thirwall, "On the Irony of Sophocles."

present the events, and the author had to draw the audience to share his perspective on the characters and events unfolding on the stage.

Three approaches to irony in the Fourth Gospel are identified according to the source of the superior knowledge that irony requires: (1) the "wink," where the author explicitly informs the reader that there is a second or fuller meaning (e.g., 11:50–52); (2) instances where the author relies upon the superior knowledge which he supplies at other places (e.g., 7:48); and (3) instances where the superior knowledge is supposed to come from sources outside the Gospel (e.g., 1:31; 11:16). Instances of irony in John cluster around themes or truths the author wished to emphasize. Wead identifies five such themes: (1) King of the Jews, (2) the origin of the Christ, (3) the superiority of Jesus to the patriarchs, (4) the destruction of the temple, and (5) irony related to discipleship. There are at times differences among these themes in the ways irony is conveyed. For example, with the first, which is developed in the passion narrative, the reader is expected to see the disparity between the "appearance" seen by the participants and the "reality" of what was actually happening. The irony of Jesus' origin, not Galilee but Bethlehem, and ultimately not Bethlehem but from God, assumes knowledge not communicated by the Gospel and often employs the unanswered question. Similarly, Jesus' superiority to the patriarchs is often communicated through an unanswered question (e.g., 4:12; 8:53). With respect to the irony that "the Jews" achieved the result they wished to avoid (the destruction of the temple) Wead offers the following interpretation of Jesus' challenge to the authorities in John 2:19,

> 'Destroy this body (in which I live) and you shall destroy also this temple (in which we stand), and I shall raise up a new temple to take its place in a short time.' Such an interpretation would apply the double meaning only to the first part of the statement, so it seems impossible to apply it to the latter part. (83)

Finally, in the instances where irony appears in passages related to discipleship, "the function of irony is observable as a tool employed subtly by the author to spur some readers to come to embrace faith in Jesus as the Christ for the first time, and to inspire believers to deeper commitments of faithfulness (20:30–31)" (84). The irony related to discipleship is at its sharpest in the reversal of sight and blindness in John 9. The authorities claim they are not blind, but "their claim to sight condemns them to responsibility for their ignorance" (86).

At the end of the chapter on irony, Wead includes an excursus on misunderstanding in which he argues that misunderstanding "is not truly a literary device, but merely a technique by which the more precise meanings and the other literary devices of the author are revealed more clearly to his readers" (88) because it cannot be separated from the signs, double meaning, and irony, which typically involve misunderstanding.[46]

Johannine irony—as elusive as it is evident—has figured prominently in later narrative criticism of the Gospel. Wead published a further analysis of "Johannine Irony as a Key to the Author-Audience Relationship in John's Gospel" in 1974,[47] and irony in John has subsequently been explored especially by Paul D. Duke and Gail R. O'Day.[48]

5. METAPHOR IN THE FOURTH GOSPEL

Moving beyond Aristotle's functional definition of metaphor, Wead defines metaphor as a literary device that depends on the reader's rejecting the literal sense and fixing on a figurative meaning. A metaphor differs from a simile: "When an author uses a simile, one draws the comparison for one's hearers. When using a metaphor, the author depends upon his or her audience to make the inference that results in the new meaning" (92). This metaphorical process may lie behind symbols because "the symbol is only possible when we arrive at the final step of the metaphorical process, and such a process has solidified into the place where the word can become a token for the second idea" (92).

The "first and most important" uses of metaphor in John are found in the "I am" sayings, although not all of these sayings are metaphorical (e.g., 4:26; 8:18 [93]). The "I am" sayings do not stand in isolation, but are part of the rich texture of the Gospel that aids in their interpretation. Wead takes issue with Rudolf Bultmann and Eduard Schweizer, who interpret the

46. For differing assessments of the role of misunderstanding in John, see Herbert Leroy, *Rätsel und Missverständnis*; Culpepper, *Anatomy of the Fourth Gospel*, 152–65; and Carson, "Understanding Misunderstandings," 59–91.

47. Wead, "Johannine Irony," 33–50.

48. Duke, *Irony in the Fourth Gospel*; and O'Day, *Revelation in the Fourth Gospel*. See also MacRae, "Theology and Irony," 83–96; Culpepper, *Anatomy of the Fourth Gospel*, 165–80; Botha, "Reopened I," 209–20; Botha, "Reopened II," 221–32; Stephen D. Moore, "Are There Impurities," 43–64; Culpepper, "Reading Johannine Irony," 193–207.

terms in the "I am" sayings as symbolic titles. Even if one is disposed to this view, the sayings require the metaphorical process of rejecting the literal meaning in favor of a figurative sense. Interpreting the sayings literally, or as "masked," "rules out the very nature by which metaphor conveys meanings" (95). Bultmann found in Hebrews 13:20 and 1 Peter 5:4 the basis for the change of metaphor to the title "good shepherd."[49] Wead rejects this line of argument, however, because it "eliminates any possibility of a historical basis for the speeches of Jesus and makes the speeches of Jesus that are found in John total constructions of the author. We cannot help but question whether Hebrews 13:20 and 1 Peter 5:4 could not more easily have been the product of the tradition behind John" (96).[50]

Wead further identifies a pattern in John that he finds in Matthew also: "It is a pattern of usage whereby the metaphor is stated or implied, and then it is followed by an 'extension' either in a short parabolic form, a sign, or a discourse" (99). In John 8:34–36, for example, we find "an illustration of the Johannine pattern: a metaphor with a parabolic form following it, which thereby extends the meaning" (99). Other examples of this pattern of a metaphor followed by an extension occur in John 3:29 (without express statement of the metaphor), 5:19–20, and 5:35. In Matthew, this pattern occurs in 5:13–15 and 15:14.

Moving on from these short extensions, Wead discusses four metaphorical discourses (παροιμίαι) in John (6:27–58; 4:8–15; 10:1–18; 15:1–8), each of which has its own characteristics and employs a different approach to the metaphor.[51] The metaphors are typically rooted in the Old Testament and daily life, with Christian elements added. The Bread of Life discourse (6:27–58) is built on an elaborate use of metaphor, with each section treating a different element of the metaphor.[52] Wead identifies seven elements of the basic metaphor, and shows how the author moves back and forth between the literal and the figurative. In spite of the similarities between the Bread of Life discourse and the living water discourse (4:8–15), there is a surprising difference between the two: "In John 6, the 'I am' reference is

49. Bultmann, *Gospel of John*, 366.

50. For recent work on the literary function of the "I am" sayings, see: Harner, *"I Am"*; Ball, *'I Am' in John's Gospel*; Williams, *I Am He*; and Porter, *John, His Gospel, and Jesus*, 120–48.

51. Thomaskutty, *Dialogue*. See also Tolmie, *Jesus' Farewell*; Moloney, "Function of John 13–17," 43–66.

52. See now Anderson, *Christology of the Fourth Gospel*; Culpepper, *Critical Readings*; and Counet, *John*, esp. 203–38.

expressed seven times; in John 4, not at all" (111). Wead therefore proposes that "the discourse is based upon the unexpressed metaphor: ἐγώ εἰμι τὸ ὕδωρ τὸ ζῶν" (111).[53] In the case of the extended discourse on the door and the good shepherd (10:1–18), we have "a saying where the meaning does not come from the story, but the meaning gives the story its significance" (118).[54] An increase in allegorical character is apparent in the discourse on the true vine (15:1–8); three metaphorical elements identify the main characters in the discourse. In spite of these differences, the four discourses share many similarities, and Jesus is the center of each of them: "The metaphorical union of concepts brings together elements from the ministry of Jesus, viewed through the lens of the evangelist's interpretation, connecting biblical themes and figures within a new synthesis of meaning" (121).

Studies of metaphor in the Gospel of John, especially the work of Jan G. van der Watt and Ruben Zimmermann, have made a distinctive contribution to Johannine scholarship in recent years.[55]

In an epilogue that has been added to this edition of *Literary Devices in John's Gospel*, the author extends the connections between John and the ancient tragedians noted in the chapter on irony. Recalling and nuancing the theory advanced by D. Butler Pratt in 1907,[56] Wead proposes that the evangelist employed patterns of Greek drama, especially in the prologue and epilogue(s) of the Gospel. These patterns reached their full development in antiquity with Euripides, who used a prologue to provide the audience with necessary information, introduce the major characters, and supply the perspective of the author on the events about to be related. The prologue was then often followed by a dialogue. The dramatists also faced the problem of how "to bring closure and meaning to events that the audience knew were not the end of the story" (125). The solution involved one or more of three methods: *deus ex machina*, an aetiological reference, and the use of a chorus (125). Wead shows how adaptations of these patterns

53. On the discourse in John 4, see: O'Day, *Revelation in the Fourth Gospel*; Boers, *Neither on This Mountain*; Maccini, *Her Testimony is True*; Day, *Woman at the Well*; Kim, *Woman and Nation*, esp. 90–115.

54. See Beutler and Fortna, *Shepherd Discourse*; Kysar, "Johannine Metaphor," 81–111; and van der Watt, "Interpreting Imagery," 272–82.

55. van der Watt, "Metaphorik," 67–80; van der Watt, *Family of the King*; Zimmermann, "Metapherntheorie," 108–33; Zimmermann, "Paradigmen," 1–34. See also Schwankl, *Licht und Finsternis*.

56. Pratt, "Gospel of John," 448–59.

are evident in John, thus reflecting its cultural setting and adaptation of yet another literary device.[57]

As one can see, *Literary Devices in John's Gospel* was ahead of its time in developing approaches to the Gospel of John that are still being pursued in contemporary scholarship. Although it explores literary devices whose functions can be understood more fully within the communication model used in narrative criticism, because Wead's work is grounded in historical criticism it also provides suggestive ideas regarding the development of the gospel tradition.

For example, Wead suggestively identifies "extensions" of metaphors in John that we may now see as artifacts of a generative process by which metaphors or images generated aphorisms or parables, discourses, or signs stories. In the course of analyzing the generative potency of aphorisms, John Dominic Crossan cites examples that "indicate the intensive development *from saying to dialogue to discourse* that took place especially with gnostic Christianity but also within those strands of catholic Christianity, such as the gospel of John."[58] Later, his work on the aphoristic saying in Luke 19:42–44b and the aphoristic story in Mark 13:2 leads him to conclude that the direction of development was from the story to the saying: "This is a salutary reminder that the movement is not always in the one direction, not always from saying to story, but sometimes in the opposite direction as well."[59] Helmut Koester argues for the same process, namely, "dialogues were initially developed in the process of the interpretation of sayings of Jesus," and offers this challenge to future scholars: "To demonstrate this for the entire text of the extensive discourses and dialogues of the Gospel of John is a task that still waits to be done."[60]

As such new lines of work on the gospel tradition and its literary devices are explored, David Wead's pioneering venture into this area will continue to serve as a significant milestone in Johannine scholarship.

57. See Brant, *Dialogue and Drama*; for a seminal exploration of the role of *anagnōrisis*, which also draws on parallels in ancient Greek drama, see the work of Larsen, *Recognizing the Stranger*.

58. Crossan, *In Fragments*, 268; emphasis original.

59. Crossan, *In Fragments*, 307.

60. Koester, *Ancient Christian Gospels*, 256–57.

INTRODUCTION

The author of John's Gospel used a number of distinctive literary devices in its construction. These literary tools are an important part of any serious study of John. They bring the author's thought patterns to the reader's attention.

John ventures into new and expressive modes of thought to make his Gospel a new world to explore. Yet some of these literary devices were not new, even to the ancient world. They also had been employed by Homer, the Greek poets, and Aristotle. Aristotle is especially important because he took the care to define and illustrate most of the ancient techniques. On the other hand, some of these devices were not so well-defined in the ancient world. These enter the work because of the message the author had to give.

They point us to the purpose of the author: he wrote a Gospel to convert and strengthen, not an artistic work to entertain. The relationship between Gospel and art shows that the art is ever secondary. The purpose of the author lies with the Christian faith. That artistic literary devices enter the work is only a testimony to the stature of the author.

I include a fitting illustration of this in my first chapter. It was not until Henry James that the definition of the literary point of view became important (ftnt.1, p. 1 Yet this does not mean that this device was not used before it was defined. In every story told, the author takes a position in relation to the story he tells. In John, the author placed himself consciously after the events looking back on them. He did not tell the story as if he was presently a part of the events. The author felt that he could relate the truth of the gospel more convincingly from this position after the resurrection. We must never lose sight of this in our discussion. The art of the Gospel is always secondary to the Gospel itself.

This literary point of view lays the foundation required for the author's other devices. The synoptic authors write presupposing the resurrection. At times, their thought and purpose as a whole demonstrate a position where the resurrection and even the church are presupposed. However, in doing this, they make no effort to place the teller of the story in this post-resurrection position. Rather, the one relating the events is placed in the event as if he were there. John's Gospel places us after the event of the resurrection; we know it and its effects. From this vantage point, John relates the story looking back on the events of the earthly life and ministry of Jesus, yet his word usage demonstrates that basic truths were not understood in connection with these events until after the resurrection of Christ.

This makes John's literary standpoint centrally important for our study. By it, the author reveals two contrasting understandings of each event: the viewpoint of those who participated in the events, and that of the apostles following the resurrection. The literary devices John uses often rely on our ability as readers of the Gospel to know more than those who participated in the events. This special knowledge is based upon our peculiar position after the resurrection.

The Johannine use of the sign (σημεῖον) employs this post-resurrection point of view. The sign is a miracle performed by Jesus in order to demonstrate a truth that leads to faith. Each sign was intended to produce faith, and John's choice of miracles for inclusion in the Gospel must be considered in this light. Not only do 20:30–31 and 21:25 expressly state this literary purpose, but also it becomes evident when one ventures into the miracles and the teaching that follows or precedes each one.

The use of σημεῖον also offers an important glimpse into the thought world of the Gospel writer. His definition of σημεῖον is peculiarly Hebrew and not closely related to the Greek conception of this term. The contrast with the Greek approach that is evident in Philo or Daniel offers another piece of evidence pointing to the Palestinian milieu as a background for this Gospel.

This dual aspect of the author's thought is emphasized in the exploration into the double-meaning words. Our research shows that the author often intended to convey two meanings with one word or series of words. The double meanings follow on the basis of standard secondary meanings usually developed through metaphors, where primary and the secondary meanings are both intended to apply.

We do not intend to espouse the philosophy of translation that all words mean all things in all contexts, as some have done recently. This idea, which seems to have stemmed from Jewish Pharisaic biblical exegesis, is to be rejected. Special care must be taken so that the meanings are not inferred where the author has not intended them.

The Johannine use of irony is another of the distinctive literary devices that rely heavily upon its literary point of view. While it cannot be denied that other New Testament writers use irony, the extent to which John uses it and the method by which he follows central themes with most of his ironic statements are unique to his Gospel. Johannine knowledge of events not mentioned in his Gospel, and the reader's supposed knowledge of these events is also implied through the evangelist's use of this device.

Another unique literary device found in the Gospel of John is connected with the use of metaphor and the related interpretative material. The "I am" passages are an important part of the theology of the Gospel, as the author centers his message in these brief statements. The metaphor by its nature is not a comparison, but a union of terms. As a literary device, the author found it useful to emphasize his conviction that the Christian message given through Jesus was reliant upon the background of the people, while also being new and unique. This uniqueness comes when we consider that the union of terminology and concepts is incomplete unless christological understanding is applied to the imagery. Often these metaphors are not expressed alone, but they follow as parts of discourses that expand their meaning.

In preparation for this work, we have considered carefully how we should most aptly describe the work being done. Hermeneutics has become a loaded term for the present theological discussion, used in both broad and narrow senses. The narrow sense connotes the science of interpretation of the Scriptures, the process by which meaning was taken from the text as applied by previous generations.

The broader, existential thrust of our present generation has enlarged this term so that the ontology of the individuals involved in the presentation also becomes a basic element in the interpretation. Those wishing to use the term in this manner have come to use it in the singular—hermeneutic—to show this distinctive change. While these quests into demythologizing have been hailed by some as very important, our purpose is not to use hermeneutic in this way.

Therefore, we have decided to use the term "literary device" as a means of describing the literary phenomenology of the biblical text, itself. Not only does this terminology explain that which we find exemplified in the Gospel of John, it also emphasizes the position of the author, as opposed to that of the interpreter, in the work of textual analysis. When dealing with the distinctive tools that the author had at his disposal, these literary devices also highlight the modes of thought by which he wished to convey his message. As these literary devices are vehicles of thought and communication, they cannot be separated from hermeneutics and the science of interpretation.

The research for this work was a part of my doctoral work done at Basel University from 1966 to 1968. This study was made possible in part by a grant from the Christian Church Educational Foundation. Most helpful guidance and insight were provided by Professor Dr. Bo Reicke. His availability and concern made our time in Basel most pleasant, and we owe him an eternal debt of gratitude.

Other than some editorial changes and the addition of the epilogue noting formal similarities with Greek tragedy and Euripides, this second edition of this work is largely unchanged from the first edition. Since its publication, however, others have picked up the research and expanded on these topics in multiple, profitable ways. One cannot help but note, for instance, the contribution of R. Alan Culpepper, whose literary work on gospel narratives has created a new epoch in literary biblical analysis. I am especially grateful to Alan for his gracious foreword to this book, situating its contribution within the larger field of Johannine studies and their development. I also thank the publishers at Wipf & Stock and the editors of the Johannine Monograph Series for including this revised edition in this important series.[61]

---

61. This book was originally published following the completion of a doctorate in theology at Basel University. The research was done at the direction of Professor Bo Reicke, with Professor Oscar Cullmann as the second reader. This book represents a revised edition of the 1970 publication, and the addition of the epilogue is entirely new and represents a new line of thinking.

CHAPTER 1

THE POST-RESURRECTION POINT OF VIEW

Often a movie or a novel will begin with an event and then move back into the past to show earlier events that preceded the opening event. This movement is necessary because the relationship between the event and its past is such that the one affects the other's meaning. The present event cannot be properly understood without knowledge of what was past, and past events are not complete without knowledge of the effects that they caused.

Such a process, involving reflection upon events of the past and their meaning, is what has produced the Gospel of John. John assumes a literary point of view in his Gospel, which allows readers to consider the life of Jesus from a point in time following the resurrection. With their knowledge of the life of Jesus and its effects, later readers are allowed to see the significance of that life in a complete perspective. This perspective governs much of John's thought and his mode of expression, allowing the narrator to choose different material, place common material in an entirely different light, and give readers valuable insights into the life of Jesus.

ANALYSIS OF THE LITERARY POINT OF VIEW

Since Henry James laid the foundations for twentieth-century literary criticism, the point of view, or *Erzählungssituation*, has become one of the most discussed areas of literary analysis. Percy Lubbock, among others of James' disciples, did important work to bring this literary device to its place of prominence.[1] Point of view shows the position where the author stands in relation to the events he is relating to his readers. It does not deal with the subject of who is talking, in spite of the fact that the author may use either

---

1. Lubbock, *Craft of Fiction*, 59–91.

the first or third person when relating what went on. Rather, it deals with the higher question of who is telling the story.

When we come to explore the question of point of view, there are three main questions Connolly poses in *A Rhetoric Case Book* that may be asked of every narration to determine the point of view.[2] Who is telling the story? From what physical point of view or angle of narration is he telling the story? From what mode, or mental point of view, is he telling the story?

Of these three, the first is the least important. However, the second and third must be properly understood if we are to gain the necessary access into the story and the meaning the author desired. The author may choose to tell the story through the eyes of a character in the event, or tell the story himself.

The physical point of view is usually limited to two authorial choices. One may either be an observer in the event (the first-person point of view), or one may present the account of a person separated from the event (the third-person point of view).[3] The first gives a feeling of immediacy; the reader is made to participate in the event. But the first-person vantage point also greatly limits the range with which the author can deal with the event. One is thereby limited to the expressions of the sensations, feelings, and thoughts of the observers.

The third-person point of view may thus lose its feeling of closeness with the reader. Immediacy is sacrificed to gain greater range of perspective, from which the author can relate the narration. The author may add later insights and meaning his characters have received through the perspective of time. He can interrupt the narrative to give pertinent details that no firsthand observer would be able to grasp.

> Are we placed before a particular scene, an occasion, at a selected hour in the lives of these people whose fortunes are to be followed? Or, are we surveying their lives from a height, participating in the privilege of the novelist—sweeping their history with a wide range of vision and absorbing a general effect? Here at once is a necessary alternative.[4]

When the author uses this latter point of view, he or she must also face another decision: determining how to include information that the firsthand observer will not know. The author may choose either to limit

2. Connolly, *Rhetoric Case Book*, 588.
3. Connolly, *Rhetoric Case Book*, 588.
4. Lubbock, *Craft of Fiction*, 66.

the narrator's knowledge, or one may insert into the narration important facts and information, which the readers need in order to understand the sequence of events properly, or the significance of particular events.[5] This "omniscient-author convention" may create an intimacy between the author and the reader as they communicate, enabling the reader's identification with the author.[6]

The mental point of view of the author is equally as important as the physical point of view. If there is to be any coherence in the story, the mental point of view must be consistent with the physical point of view. The author must make his or her mental analysis of the situation agree with the point of view expressed physically, as authorial sense-perceptions and thoughts affect the course and progress of the story. They determine the predominant tone and attitude of the narration. According to Connolly, a man must speak through his own mind with his own purpose and understanding as it affects the story.[7]

In terms of John's narrative, this means that our author cannot reveal a post-resurrection physical point of view and yet maintain a naïveté to the theological meaning of the theological events he relates. As he explicates his mental point of view as a theologian, he must deal with the events theologically and from the significance of the physical point of view.

THE AUTHOR'S STORYTELLER: THE BELOVED DISCIPLE

When we turn to the first of these three questions that Connolly suggests, we find that the text itself answers the question of who is telling the story. But this comes only at the very end of the work in John 21:24: "This is the disciple who testifies to these things and who wrote them down, and we know his testimony is true."[8] By associating himself with this disciple, the author has very carefully given himself access to the events of the life of Christ. He is an eyewitness or had acquaintance with an eyewitness of all that has happened. Beginning with 1:35–42, the author includes, in addition to Andrew, the witness of an unnamed disciple of John the Baptist. Through the account of the disciple known to the high priest (18:15–16)

5. Lubbock, *Craft of Fiction*, 66.

6. Harvey, *Art of George Elliot*, 19.

7. Connolly, *Rhetoric Case Book*, 589.

8. Unless otherwise indicated, the primary version of Scripture used in this book is the NIV.

and the disciple whom Jesus loved (13:24, 19:26, 20:2, 21:20), the narrator has been very careful to have a witness available. The exceptions—such as the trial before Pilate, where it is unlikely that a witness was present—are rare. We cannot with assurance unite these figures to form one personality, but we can see in all these figures the presence of a witness to the events, who relates them to us as readers. Thus, the author includes witnesses to events in the narrative, implying firsthand acquaintance with them.

THE PHYSICAL POINT OF VIEW

This rightly brings us to Connolly's second question: from what physical point of view or angle of narration is the author telling the story? This question as it relates to the Gospel of John provides a basic difference between John and the Synoptics. John uses the third-person point of view in contrast to the writers of the Synoptics, who use the first person. While the Johannine author claims to be a participant in the events, he very carefully separates himself from the events. "However clear it is that he was an eyewitness of the life of the Lord, it is no less clear that he looks back upon it from a distance."[9] While we see the events through his eyes, we are carefully guided to see them more from the position that the writer now holds rather than earlier perspectives. The author is thus able to view all from above and to see the whole panorama of the life of Jesus—including original events and their later significance.

We can best illustrate this by comparing the way Luke and John treat the incomplete knowledge of the disciples before the resurrection. Luke 24:4–6 shows the perplexity of the disciples at the empty tomb, followed by the admonition of the angels that they should remember that Jesus had said he would raise from the dead. Verse 8 shows their remembrance of the words of Jesus, but all of this is involved with the individual sense experience of the disciples at the time following the resurrection.[10] Jesus explains the Scriptures to the disciples later in the chapter so that, in light of the resurrection, they might understand their true significance. In John, however, this new understanding of the resurrection is brought back into the text and applied to the narrated events so that the reader can see not only the earlier imperfect understanding of the disciples, but also the later complete understanding as it developed after the resurrection (John 2:21–22;

9. Westcott, *Gospel*, xxxvi.
10. Michel, "μιμνήσκομαι," 4:681.

THE POST-RESURRECTION POINT OF VIEW 5

12:15–16). In Luke, we are limited to the understanding of the characters as it was evident at the time. In John, we are not so limited; however, we are placed in a position where we can understand the more complete theological perspective that the events came to hold for the church.

> The conception of the purpose of John in his gospel marks a difference of standpoint between the earlier evangelists and the last. John is anxious to prove the truth of Jesus' physical life and ministry, and at a time when He had been the object of Christian worship for more than half a century. Christian reflection and Christian experience had reached a doctrine of the Person of Christ which had not been clearly thought out by Christians in the first enthusiastic devotion to their Master. The Synoptists draw a picture of Jesus as viewed by his contemporaries; the Fourth Gospel is a profound study of that picture, bringing into full view what may not have been clearly discerned at the first.[11]

Lonergan also brings out this view of the Christ as it is found in John. He cites three schemata through which the New Testament writers view the Christ in their writings. The *schema prospectivum*, chosen by the synoptic writers, is what we have described as the first-person point of view. Second, he describes the *schema retrospectivum*, which views Jesus as the exalted Son of God seated on the right hand of God, ruling the present world. This view is found pervasively in Paul. The third viewpoint, the *schema retrospectivum inversum*, shows Jesus as a man but does not consider his life as limited to the earthly life. This schema also views the life of Jesus both in its pre-existence and its present glorification and reign. This latter he finds both in John and occasionally in Paul.[12]

John's panoramic view of the life of Christ is indicated with his first words in the prologue—a marked difference between this Gospel and the others. While Matthew sets forth an earthly lineage, and Luke limits himself to that which Jesus began to do and teach, John's vision of the life of Jesus takes us beyond the limits of earthly existence to the very beginning of the cosmos, when the Word existed with God. Thus, we are led to expect that the author will not be limited in his picture of the life of Jesus. The author of the Fourth Gospel does not choose to limit himself, as have the other evangelists. He does not disappoint us.

We thus find four important passages that bring this to our attention:

11. Bernard, *Critical and Exegetical Commentary*, 1:cxxxv.
12. Lonergan, *De Verbo Incarnato*, 23.

2:17 His disciples remembered [ἐμνήσθησαν] that it is written, "Zeal for your house will consume me."

2:22 After he was raised from the dead, his disciples recalled [ἐμνήσθησαν] what he had said. Then they believed the Scripture and the words that Jesus had spoken.

12:16 At first his disciples did not understand all this. Only after Jesus was glorified did they realize [ἐμνήσθησαν] that these things were written about him and they had done these things to him.

20:9 They still did understand from Scripture [οὐδέπω γὰρ ᾔδεισαν τὴν γραφὴν] that Jesus had to rise from the dead.

In each of these passages of Scripture, the importance of the post-resurrection point of view of the Gospel is emphasized.[13] The writer stands beyond the resurrection and looks back upon the event. He emphasizes the inability of the apostles to understand the events as they were happening. (cf. Mark 8:17–18). Even when the apostles went into the empty tomb, they did not grasp what had happened. They develop the proper understand through their contact with the Risen Lord. As McCool shows, only then do they comprehend fully what had happened.[14]

The third-person point of view in John becomes quite clear. He does not wish to limit himself to the events of Jesus' earthly life, nor should the events of the earthly life of Jesus be understood merely as the disciples understood them at the time. The fuller understanding that comes with the perspective of the resurrection is thus necessary for a proper understanding of the events later reported.

Let us then turn to see how this "omniscient author" uses the advantages he has chosen to illuminate the text before us. He is not as subtle as the twentieth-century author would attempt to be. Most of the passages where the author intrudes are clear.

The author considers the situation in which Jesus lived to be important. In recognition that his audience might not be acquainted with the customs and times of Jesus' life in Palestine, he gives us many insights into such conditions. Thus, we are informed about the place where John was baptizing (1:28), the Jewish customs regarding purification (2:6), the strained relations that existed between Jews and Samaritans (4:9), the belief of some of the Jewish leaders who chose to remain secret because of their

---

13. Schnackenburg, *Das Johannesevangelium*, 167.

14. McCool, *Introduction*, 35–36.

desire to hold their positions (12:42–43), and the burial customs of the Jews (19:40).

The author notes numerous instances where the disciples' understanding (or their lack of it) is evident. In John 2:11, the disciples' belief is witnessed as a result of the sign that Jesus did. Their belief and understanding are pictured in a continuing state of growth. Through the office of the omniscient author, John shows us that they did not understand what Jesus told Judas when Judas went out to betray him (13:28–29), they did not understand the teaching concerning the resurrection until after it had happened (20:9), and they did not recognize Jesus at first when he appeared to them on the shores of the Lake of Galilee (21:4).

The author also includes many little notes which give us insight into the meaning of the words of Jesus as they were later (and, more correctly, the author believes) understood.[15] John 2:22 notes that Jesus was really speaking about the temple of his body when he referred to the destruction of the temple. When the disciples thought that Jesus said that Lazarus was recovering (κεκοίμηται), John tells us that he really meant the man had died (11:13). Jesus spoke of the coming of the Holy Spirit before the Spirit was actually given (7:39). The author informs us of Jesus' prophecy concerning the manner of his death (12:33), the reason for Jesus not allowing all of the disciples to be considered clean (13:11), and the false conception that the writer of the Gospel should live until Jesus' return (21:23).

Another practice revealing the omniscient-author convention deals with the historical information the author gives us about the characters. This information often comes before the event involved takes place. In 11:2, the author informs us that "this Mary, whose brother Lazarus now lay sick, was the same one who poured perfume on the Lord and wiped his feet with her hair." But Mary does not perform this service of love until 12:4. This total lack of concern for the orderly procession of the events would be decried by the modern author.[16] John also shows us that Judas was a

---

15. Mussner, *Historical Jesus*, 44, 46.

16. Again, John is not a modern author. For this reason, we have limited ourselves from many of the modern nuances and discussions concerning the point of view. That which is the modern writer's prerogative was not understood or intended by the ancient author. There seems to be much discussion among the makers of current literary tradition about this point. The problem that has developed is simple: by the standards of the first part of the twentieth century, even the novels of the eighteenth century cease to be good works. If the reader should be interested in this discussion, he might refer to the position and bibliography presented by Booth, *Rhetoric of Fiction*, 211.

thief and took from the bag (12:6). In 18:14, he reverses the procedure. The reference is made to that which has previously happened: "Caiaphas was the one who had previously advised the Jews that it would be good if one man died for the people." He speaks in reference to the note previously added in 11:52–53.

THE MENTAL POINT OF VIEW

The mental point of view is a bit harder to grasp because the reader cannot proceed to pick out isolated verses that show the author breaking into the text itself in order to reveal his mental stance. However, proceeding with the assumption that the author has composed a coherent work, we can only test the hypothesis that the mental point of view must be the same as the physical point of view.

If we are to expect such coherence in the mental attitude of the author, then we should expect to find embedded in the text the understanding of the resurrection and the doctrine of salvation that resulted from it. He must bring his theological understanding of the events of the life of Christ into congruity with his theological position after the resurrection in such a way that the meaning of the text becomes clear. John pictures Jesus as teaching his contemporaries with the total effect of his life and work in view. Those who were earlier taught by Jesus did not and could not grasp the full significance of his teachings.

The incomplete understanding of the disciples is stated expressly twice. When Jesus speaks to Peter at the foot washing, and Peter does not wish to be served by his master, Jesus answers, "You do not realize now what I am doing, but later you will understand" (13:7). This sets the teaching of Jesus within the proper mental point of view. The author's position of full understanding exposes ironically the disciples' original lack of understanding. The passion of Christ and the events resulting immediately from it are thus necessary for understanding properly the events in the life of Jesus.

The other passage we would cite regarding the disciples' lack of understanding is 16:29–30: "Then Jesus' disciples said, 'Now you are speaking clearly and without figures of speech. Now we can see that you know all things and that you do not need to have anyone ask you questions. This makes us believe that you came from God.'"

In commenting on this, Bultmann comments on Jesus' superior knowledge, and how the disciples now understand that he does not speak in riddles but is openly declaring to them the plain truth.[17] The Synoptics also record this lack of understanding on the part of the disciples (Mark 8:17–18; Luke 18:34; 24:6, 8). Finding such misunderstandings among the disciples after the Parable of the Sower, Matthew records Jesus as not only giving the disciples a further explanation, but also stating that such a lack of understanding among the people was to fulfill the prophecy of Isaiah (Matt 13:10–16).

The mental point of view of John has allowed him to choose material that the other writers did not use and to present it with the confidence that his readers, also sharing his post-resurrection point of view, would understand what was said in its true light.[18] This mental point of view, which has guided the author's choice and presentation of material, can best be seen in the presentation of the coming of the Holy Spirit. Jesus declares that "whoever believes in me, as the Scripture has said, streams of living water will flow from within him" (7:38). The following verse reveals the author's point of view when he says, "By this he meant the Spirit, whom those who believed on him were later to receive. Up to that time the Spirit had not been given, since Jesus had not yet been glorified." With the knowledge that the believer could not understand the doctrine of the Spirit until the Spirit was given, Jesus continues to teach concerning it until finally he breathes on the disciples and they receive the Holy Spirit (20:22).

But the promise is that the Holy Spirit shall be the possession of all believers. Not only does the Pentecost tradition in Acts teach us this, but also John 3:5. Thus it becomes apparent that full understanding of the teaching of Jesus comes when believers view the teaching from the time following the resurrection, and also Pentecost.

Bound up with this promise is the author's position that Jesus not only left a moral teaching, but that he also lived and taught with a body of followers in mind who would come to understand his mission more fully after his death and resurrection (17:20). These believers would be affected by a soteriological perspective quite different from the conventional Judaism of which Jesus himself was a part. This transformed perspective could only take effect through Christ's atoning suffering on the cross—his paradoxical glorification. So Jesus lived as a Jew, but presented a new covenant from God apart from humanly devised religion. He presented this new way so

17. Bultmann, *Theologie des Neuen Testaments*, 395.

18. Bultmann, *Gospel of John*, 588–89; Dahl, "Anamnesis," 69–95; Kiefer, *Die Hirtenrede*, 41.

that those who believed on him might come into it—but its full character could only be envisioned after he was gone.

When the author relates the account of Jesus' teaching Nicodemus in John 3, the question of Nicodemus's understanding becomes unimportant. The fact of the Gospel is that Nicodemus did not understand what was taught to him. The author records two statements from Nicodemus following his introduction. "How can a man be born when he is old?" Nicodemus asked. "Surely he cannot enter a second time into his mother's womb to be born!" (3:4); "How can this be?" (3:9). The crucial question becomes for us not "what did Nicodemus understand?" but "what is John wishing his readers to understand?" E. Hoskyns observes: "He did not, however, discourse with Nicodemus, but to him and through him to the readers of the gospel, for Nicodemus soon disappears in the darkness he had selected for his visit."[19]

The author assumes that the readers are familiar with the terms of salvation and baptism as they are used in terms of regeneration. Certainly, this was not a new subject within the early Christian movement.[20] The Epistles used it freely (1 Pet 1:22–23; 2:2; 3:18–22; Titus 3:5), but John presents Jesus as teaching doctrine that would only be fully understood at a later date. The commentator's question, "What did Nicodemus understand?", thus becomes relatively unimportant, as the text states that he did not understand. How the conversation may have proceeded through the remainder of the evening, we do not know.

In 6:51–58, John records the Jews' inability to understand Jesus' statement regarding the eating of his flesh. Jesus' answer does not seem to clarify an answer to their question; rather, it is a further statement of the truth that produced the question. One of the chief arguments used by those who do not feel this passage can be interpreted in relation to the Lord's Supper is this: "How could the listeners understand?" John indicates that they did not. Rather, he assumes that readers have the correct answer to the question—one that those hearing him in the story could not imagine. They asked, but could not accept the answer, for the full understanding of both depended upon the future events. The author's point of view thus allows him to present the teachings of Jesus in this way.

19. Hoskyns, *Fourth Gospel*, 203; cf. also Dodd, *Interpretation*, 338. Of course, Nicodemus comes around later and is presented as standing up for Jesus among the Jewish leaders in chapter 7 and at the cross in chapter 19.

20. Hoskyns, *Fourth Gospel*, 214.

This same practice appears when Jesus teaches about the Good Shepherd in John 10. The disciples misunderstand, so Jesus must explain, referencing the good shepherd who lays down his life for his sheep, an obvious allusion to his death and resurrection. Hoskyns says, "The parable is complete only when it has born witness to the death and resurrection of Jesus." In similar fashion, the significance of the feeding of the five thousand is not exhausted until the bread is expounded as the flesh which Jesus will give for the life of the world, and the feeding which provides life is declared to be the eating of His body and the drinking of His blood."[21]

In 7:33–36, we have the statement concerning the return to the Father, which the Jews again misunderstand. These same words come in much the same fashion to the disciples, who also misunderstand later in the narrative (14:19). Jesus is obviously (to us, the reader) referencing his death and resurrection, but the teaching is only understandable in light of those events having taken place.

Thus, there is adequate evidence in John's Gospel to accept the mental point of view that is coherent with the physical point of view. The physical to a large extent determines the mental, but both are coherent with one another and complement one another.

THEOLOGICAL IMPLICATIONS

An exploration into the literary point of view also reveals the overall unity of the Gospel. Following the unity of grammatical style—as has been demonstrated by Schweizer, Ruckstuhl, and Noack—the literary point of view becomes another factor that speaks for the unitive composition of the Gospel.[22]

If the author employed other sources, written or oral, they were so molded by him, and he was so selective in his choice of material, that he composed a work distinctly his own. There could be no mere compilation of material that did not involve its complete integration by the author before its inclusion.[23]

Another problem upon which the study of the literary point of view in John throws light on is posited by Ernst Käsemann. He points to the fact

---

21. Hoskyns, *Fourth Gospel*, 367–68.

22. See Schweizer, *Ego Eimi*; Ruckstuhl, *Die Literarische Einheit*; and Noack, *Zur Johanneischen Tradition*.

23. Bultmann, "Johannesevangelium," 3:843.

that we come face to face with Johannine theology and must deal with the theology of the Johannine church.[24] This problem—that of *gemeindetheologie*—becomes thorny in the present discussion. Two basic truths form the background of the problem in the Gospel of John. According to Dodd, "For unquestionably the tradition, in all its forms intends to refer to an historical episode closely dated sub Pontio Pilato apart from which (there is the implication) there would have been no church to shape or hand down the tradition."[25]

Against this first truth we have observed from the Gospel that the second truth comes with equal force upon the problem. Westcott says,

> In dwelling on such aspects of Christian teaching, it is clear that the evangelist is measuring the interval between the first imperfect views of the Apostles as to the Kingdom of God and that just ideal, which he had been allowed to shape under the teaching of the Paraclete, through disappointments and disasters.[26]

Thus the question is clear: Is the doctrine from the Gospel of John the doctrine Jesus taught, or the doctrine the church developed after Jesus was departed from the earth?"

Surprisingly, the question above is not only clear to us, but the evangelist himself wrestled with it, too. Within his post-resurrection point of view, the evangelist asserts that those things Jesus did and said could only be properly understood in the light of the Christ events. Thus, the apostolic community claims to be divinely gifted with authority and perspectives opened by the Holy Spirit, reflected also in their writings. According to Haenchen, there is no distinction between the teaching of Jesus and that of the apostles following the resurrection. The attempt to answer this question of the propriety of *gemeindetheologie* thus comes through the author's claim to authority. He does this in two ways: through the claim of the eyewitness reports of the apostles, and through the claim to the unfailing guidance of the Holy Spirit.

We have seen the instances where the author notes that a disciple was present to witness the events in the life of Jesus. The claim for the eyewitness report may be said to be a claim for apostolic authority. John 1:14 reads, "And the Word became flesh and lived for a while among us and we have seen [ἐθεασάμεθα] his glory." The emphasis upon "we" in this passage

24. Käsemann, *Exegetische Versuche*, 180.

25. Dodd, *Historical Tradition*, 7.

26. Westcott, *Gospel*, xxxvii.

and the "we all" in verse 16 are not without significance. Von Harnack is correct when he states that the use of the aorist ἐθεασάμεθα here refers to the understanding of John and his contemporaries that their memory was guided by the Holy Spirit.[27]

Whether we consider ἐκεῖνος to be referring to the author of the Gospel or another, 19:35 must refer to an eyewitness account. "There is a similar 'we' in 21:24 which emphasizes the importance of the testimony of the veracious eyewitnesses and adds, 'we know that his witness is true'—the Church sets its seal upon the veracity of its spokesman."[28] The eyewitness tradition of the Gospel thus provides a concrete basis for the authoritative speech of the author.

The apostolic witness relates both to the historicity and the transmission of the evidence. The claim of the special authority of the Holy Spirit is ever present before the writer, as John presents the Holy Spirit in order to emphasize the Spirit's work in relation to truth and proper interpretation. "But the Counselor, the Holy Spirit, whom the Father will send in my name, will teach you all things and will remind you of everything I have said to you" (14:26); "But when he, the Spirit of truth, comes, he will guide you into all truth" (16:13). This promise of divine direction is brought to its completion in 20:22, when the disciples receive the Holy Spirit. Thus, not only did the disciples have access to the Holy Spirit, but they found that the Spirit was their proper guide to the interpretation of Jesus' ministry. Their remembrance is not only a simple remembrance of the events, but at the same time the understanding of those events as guided by the Holy Spirit.[29] The author intended these passages for the understanding of his apostolic authority in the recording of the events.

In summary, we should emphasize the importance of the point of view of the author. The Scripture passages that note the theology of the disciples as it developed after the resurrection of Jesus point out this third-person point of view of the author. From this point in time following the resurrection of Jesus, the author was able to remove himself from the events, and yet in the end able to associate himself once more. He is able to bring to bear the truth on each of these events in the life of Jesus, which became its ultimate significance. He is thus able to deal with the events that would have been largely unintelligible without the passion of Christ, for he has

27. von Harnack, "Das 'Wir,'" 107–8.

28. Barrett, *Gospel*, 119.

29. Haenchen, "Der Vater," 214.

confidence that his readers know more than the participants in the events themselves knew.

The distinctive literary devices that John uses gain their shape in large measure from the author's post-resurrection point of view. We shall proceed to discuss these devices in the remainder of this work.

CHAPTER 2

THE JOHANNINE SIGN

The unique word the writer of the Fourth Gospel has chosen to express the miracles of Jesus may never have come to the attention of many readers of the English Bible. In the King James Version, σημεῖον is translated as "sign" only four times (John 2:18; 4:48; 6:30; 20:30), while no fewer than thirteen times the term is translated by the less expressive word, "miracle."

Our study of this term is meaningful, not only because it shows a marked difference in the approach taken by the evangelist in contrast to that taken by the Synoptics, but also because this word seems to provide a key to understanding the background of the vocabulary used by the author. C. H. Dodd has rightly recognized the importance of this word in his *Interpretation of the Fourth Gospel.*[1] However, we believe he is wrong in his choice of background for the interpretation of the Gospel of John as a whole. Our research has shown that the greatest part of the background for the Gospel is from the Old Testament. The use of σημεῖον in John does not display a fitting parallel with the uses we find in the Hermetic literature, the Mandaean writings, or Philo. Thus, it seems a strain to identify these sources as the background for the vocabulary of the author.

THE BACKGROUND OF Σημεῖον

Many classical uses of the word are of little interest to us. Σημεῖον was used to describe a seal or confirmation, an identifying inscription, a flag of a group, or any signal. If we should compare John's use with that found in the classical Greek writings, by far the most interesting is that which involves

---

1. Dodd has made the Book of Signs the designation for a major part of the Gospel of John in his book, *Interpretation of the Fourth Gospel.*

15

the omen.[2] The Greeks believed that the omen was one of the chief methods Greek gods used to make their will known. In this way, the gods revealed to humans the outcome of future events. An omen came through an event, often associated with birds. The event was interpreted by a prophet (μαντική), that is, a person specially endowed by the gods to interpret their omens. These prophets were not always sane,[3] but their interpretations were nonetheless presented as the words of the gods. Socrates implies that the sign was of great effect in his life.[4] Diodorus relates a sign in which an eagle fell upon an altar to attempt to capture a pigeon being offered, ironically becoming an offering itself. Then the prophet was then called to deliver the message of the gods by means of interpreting the events.[5] The Greek sign thus had no meaning without the interpretation, nor could interpreters bring their message without citing the event.

The Stoics and Epicureans developed another usage to the word, one in which σημεῖον became a technical logical term. This usage describes a logical argument, which presents an observable basis from which one could reason by inference to that which was not observable.[6]

The Old Testament Background

To begin our study of the Old Testament usage, it is wise to turn to the LXX. Here we find seven words translated σημεῖον: mophet, nes, tiqwah, mo'ed, mas'et, taw, 'oth, and the Aramaic equivalent of the latter 'at. Of these terms, 'at is by far the most important, always being translated as σημεῖον. The translations of 'oth in the Old Testament fall into three broad categories, in addition to those cases where the term is used as a mere indication, or a flag, or as an identifying standard.

A. The use of σημεῖον as a reminder or memorial (positively) and a warning (negatively) becomes quite common in the Old Testament. The positive emphasis calls attention to the word or action of God in the past so that the action of God will be remembered.[7] It is used this way with reference to the rainbow (Gen 9:12–13, 17), the Passover (Exod 13:9, 16),

2. Rengstorf, "σημεῖον," 201–3.

3. Plato, Phaedrus, 244c.

4. Plato, Apology 40 a, b, c.

5. Formesyn, "Le Sèmeion," 865.

6. Formesyn, "Le Sèmeion," 862.

7. Dahl, "Anamnesis," 72–73.

the Sabbath (Exod 31:13, 17; Ezek 20:6), the words of Moses (Deut 11:18), the twelve great stones in the Jordan (Josh 4:6), and the Jewish colony in Egypt (Isa 19:20).

The negative emphasis of the memorial becomes a warning. The action of God is meant to warn those who offend him. Numbers 17:10 (25 in the LXX) speaks of a "sign for the rebels to make an end to their murmurings against me, lest they die." This reference stands as a warning. Numbers 26:10 also uses σημεῖον this way, although the Hebrew equivalent is not 'oth, but *nes*.

The symbolic actions of the prophets may also be considered signs in this regard. Three events in Numbers are called signs: the hammering of the censors into covers for the altar (16:30), placing Aaron's rod before the ark (17:10; LXX 17:25), and the opening of the earth to receive the company with Korah as they strove again against Moses (26:10). These actions symbolized the fates of those who stood against Moses and Aaron, thus opposing the will of the Lord. These signs stood as warnings to later generations regarding the importance of faith and faithfulness.

In the same manner, the children of Isaiah and Hosea are named at the command of the Lord. In both instances, the names of the children stand as warnings to Israel that they should turn from the folly of their own ways (Isa 8:18; Hos 1:2–8). We might also note the same phenomenon with regard to Isaiah's nakedness (Isa 20:3) and several of Ezekiel's symbolic actions (Ezek 4:3, for example). However, the symbolic actions of the prophet and the sign should not be considered synonymous. The concepts only come together, as both serve as reminders or as warnings. There are many signs in the Old Testament that are not symbolic actions (Isa 7:14, for example) and many symbolic actions that are not signs.

B. In Exodus, the sign is presented in a different perspective, as the sign is intended to give legitimacy to the one who comes from God. Moses comes with signs to prove himself to the children of Israel (Exod 4:8–9). When he turns to present his demands to Pharaoh, the Pharaoh answers: "Prove yourself by working a miracle." The LXX here rightly translates *mophet* as σημεῖον, understanding that this as a demand for legitimation. Then follow the series of plagues, which are meant to demonstrate beyond a doubt that God's demand that the children of Israel be freed from the land of Egypt is to be heeded. The signs have a negative effect upon the heart of Pharaoh. The sign is such that one must either accept or reject it; for Pharaoh, there is no middle ground.

The Exodus period produces a new union of terms.[8] "Sign and won-der" are bound together in an effective unity to refer to the Exodus event. Beginning with Deuteronomy and continuing through the Psalms and the prophets of the post-exilic period, σημεῖα καὶ τέρατα refers to the Exodus miracles.

The wide range of texts that use σημεῖα καὶ τέρατα show us these miracles were fulfilling the expectation of Exodus 10:1–2, that they should be a witness to posterity. The terminology was used by later Judaism to express their Messianic hope.[9] Sirach 36:6 calls on God to renew this ac-tion that would bring about the Messianic age. The terminology recalls the Exodus period. (Note especially Deut 4:34; 7:19; 26:8; where the mighty hand and outstretched arm are joined with the signs and wonders.) There was a strong feeling in pre-Christian Judaism that the Messianic era would be very much like the Mosaic era.[10]

This "sign-and-wonder" union calls forth two aspects of meaning. First, the Exodus signs were wonders; that is, miraculous. Second, a sign need not be miraculous; it is simply meant to authenticate. The sign is thus miraculous as it relates to the revelation of God's workings in the world, and the action and the interpretation cannot be separated. Carl Keller, in his Basler dissertation, connects 'oth very closely with the divine, concern-ing its origin.[11] Therefore, 'oth is rarely used without its position in relation to the word of God, whose word and action thus become one. They cannot be separated. Without the word, the action has no meaning; without the action, the word has no authenticity.[12]

This connection between the word of God and the event the word authenticates brings a close connection between the word, the sign, and the prophet. The word comes to the prophet, and the sign becomes the authen-tication of the prophet's mission. Thus, authentic signs imply the office of the authentic prophet. "We are given no miraculous signs; no prophets are left, and none of us knows how long this will be" (Ps 74:9).

C. The emphasis is still upon the authentication of the word of the prophets; however, in this third set of uses, σημεῖον serves as a guarantor of the future. Isaiah 38:7–8 best illustrates this meaning: "This is the Lord's

8. Rengstorf, "σημεῖον," 219.

9. Rengstorf, "σημεῖον," 243; also Ziener, "Weisheitsbuch," 406.

10. Jeremias, "Μωϋσῆς," 867.

11. Keller, *Das Wort*, 14.

12. Keller, *Das Wort*, 177.

sign to you that the Lord will do what he has promised: I will make the shadow cast by the sun go back the ten steps it has gone down on the stairway of Ahaz." While the emphasis remains upon the authentication of the prophet's word, in this series of uses a σημεῖον serves as a future omen. The word of God is given, and a subsequent event later authenticates the word that has been given. The new element found is the increasing emphasis upon the future time of the completion of the sign.

The event may be miraculous, although it need not be. Indeed, the staying of the sun from its movement must be considered miraculous (2 Kgs 19:29; Isa 37:30), but the call that the enemy might give (1 Sam 14:10) and the death of both of the sons of Eli on the same day (1 Sam 2:34) need not be. The key to their use is that they are events that have been foretold and could only be known beforehand by divine knowledge. The one seeing the sign receives the assurance that the word of God has come through the prophet.

This use of σημεῖον as an omen (vorzeichen in German) utilizes the factor of time. The indication of "when" by a sign appears to be used first in 1 Samuel 10:6–7: "The Spirit of the Lord will come upon you in power, and you will prophesy with them and you will be changed into a different person. Once these signs are fulfilled, do whatever your hand finds to do for God is with you." As the importance of the apocalyptic arises in the prophets, it naturally follows that this element in the omen should be used to indicate the coming of the last days. In this respect, two courses are taken. In Isaiah 55:13, the everlasting sign that is given is the restoration of all to its perfect order, thorns shall become cypress and briers myrtle. In Joel 2:30 (LXX 3:3) a further apocalyptic expansion shows that the "when" of these eschatological events is to be known by the signs in the heavens and on earth.

This use of σημεῖον differs from the classical Greek use of the omen. To the Hebrew mind, the word of God comes first, and then the sign is given to authenticate the word. In the classical sign, the event or sign comes first. Then the μαντική must come and use his divine knowledge to interpret the message that the gods had given in the sign.[13] The classical prophet often spoke in platitudes with no check before the event to certify the authenticity of his message. The element of authentication, so strong in the Jewish concept, is lacking in the classical Greek concept. In the Hebrew sign, the word of God came first and was presented. Then the prophet would predict

13. Formesyn, "Le Sèmeion," 880.

an event that could be known only through divine knowledge given to the prophet. The demonstration that God had given the prophet a divine message to show a future event was considered proof that God had also revealed God's message previously to the prophet.

Before departing from the Old Testament, we should also note the prophet Daniel, where we have the most important example of the classical sign found in the Old Testament. While σημεῖον is not found in connection with the text, the classical sign of God's workings in the world as illustrated in the Joseph narratives is also displayed here. When the hand comes to write on the wall before Belshazzar, he immediately recognized the event as a sign. He calls the "astrologers, the Chaldeans, and the soothsayers" (μαντική). When these failed to interpret the sign, the queen recommends that Daniel be called. Here we find one of the finest expositions of the Greek prophet (μαντική) available to us in any writing:

> There is a man in your kingdom who has the spirit of the holy gods in him. In the time of your father he was found to have insight and intelligence and wisdom like that of the gods. King Nebuchadnezzar, your father—your father the king, I say, appointed him chief of the magicians, enchanters, astrologers and diviners. This man, Daniel, whom the king called Belteshazzar, was found to have a keen mind and knowledge and also the ability to interpret dreams, explain riddles, and solve difficult problems. Call for Daniel, and he will tell you what the writing means. (Dan 5:11–12)

Daniel is then brought in, and the interpretation of the sign is given.[14]

However, as with the classical usage in Genesis, the word from God is not known by the people who receive the sign until the interpretation was given by Daniel (or by Joseph). Both of these illustrations thus come to us when the Hebrews are in a strange culture. It is in such contexts that God works, even through the environment and religion of the strange people to show that he truly is God over all the nations.

The Background in Qumran

The uses of 'oth are carried over into the writings of Qumran. In 1QH 15:20, 'oth is used as a reminder to generations that shall follow. "All them that

---

14. The Aramaic of Daniel is closer to the Greek interpretation of the sign than the Greek of the LXX and Theodotion. The latter seems to translate the Greek meaning of the sign out of the text.

hate Thee hast Thou prepared to wreak great judgments upon them in the sight of all Thy creatures, to serve as a sign and a token forever, to make known to all men Thy glory and strength."[15] Here, the sense is again that of warning, for the creatures have been ordained for great chastisements. We see most clearly that the glory of God is revealed in the sign that comes.

The authentication of the one who shows the signs is also in the writing of Qumran. In 1QS 3:14, the spirit that inhabits a man is to be identified by the works the man does in his lifetime. These works are signs. We can see that the divine element has receded into the background, only affecting the actions of the man. There is no special, individual event as before, but the general behavior of a man is considered as that which identifies whether he has the divine spirit within him or not.

The eschatological use is also found within such writings as 1QS 10:4, and especially in 1Q27 1:15. In the latter passage, there is an event by which the "when" of the eschatological future can be known. The other uses of 'oth in the Qumran writings are involved with a standard or flag, and are found largely in the War Scroll.

The Background in Philo

In Philo, we find the expected union of the philosophical with the biblical. Σημεῖον is used to mean a point or dot, as opposed to a line or a surface. The Stoic use of the term, whereby an argument proceeds from a demonstrable known to an undemonstrable unknown, is also found here. Philo did not hesitate to use forms of the cognate verbs σημαίνω (De posteritate Caini ISS, De somnis I:65, 85, 87) and σημειοῦσθαι. (The latter is used in De specialibus legibus IV:110 in a passage parallel in thought to De specialibus legibus IV:106 where σημεῖον is used.) Philo uses σημεῖον to express his union with Platonic thought. He uses a name of an object or person to symbolize the meaning that thing had in the ideal world. "For by His own supremely manifest and far-shining Reason God makes both of them, both the original of the mind, which in symbolic language he calls 'heaven' and the original of sense-perception, to which by a figure (σημεῖον) he gave the name to 'earth'" (Leg. All. 1:21).

C. H. Dodd also notes that σημεῖον and σύμβολον are used in the same context.[16] Not only are these words found together in Leg. All. 1:21 (quoted

15. 1QH 15:20.
16. Dodd, Interpretation, 141–42.

above), but also *Leg. All.* 1:59, 120 and *Quis rer. div. heres sit* 198. The cognate σημαίνω appears with σύμβολον in *Leg. All.* 11:15. In all of these cases, the words are used to bring out the meaning of names allegorically, and are intended to be that of the ideal heavenly world.

> Again had many persons bestowed names on things, they would inevitably have been incongruous and ill-matched, different persons imposing them on different principles, whereas the naming by one man was bound to bring about harmony between name and thing, and the name given was sure to be a symbol, the same for all men, of any object to which the name was attached or of the meaning (σημαινομένου) attaching to the name. (*Legum all.* 11:15)

Philo's philosophy applies σημεῖον and σύμβολον to names and the symbolic or allegorical meaning derived from them. They never apply to events.

Philo presents his Platonic ideal clearly in the theology of the sign. To him, the sign is to be interpreted through divine insight into the meaning of the name.

> In accordance with these distinctions [σημαινόμενον] the Sacred Guide gave a perfectly clear and lucid interpretation of the appearances which come under the first description, inasmuch as the intimations given by God through these dreams were of the nature of plain oracles. (*De somnis* 11:3)

Such divine wisdom is also attributed to Abraham (*De Abrahamo* 60) or comes through "the gift of keen mental sight" (*De vita Mosis* 1:188). Philo speaks to us through such insight.

One of the most illustrative passages showing the difference between Philo's understanding of the sign and that which is found in the Old Testament comes in his comments on a passage from the Old Testament where the word "sign" is actually used. In *De spec. legibus* IV. 137–38, the symbolic action of binding the law "upon the hand and having them shaking before our eyes" is explained. The hand is considered the "symbol of action." The remaining part seems puzzling to Philo, for he says, "Of what they are a sign he has not definitely stated because, I believe, they are a sign not of one thing but of many, practically of all the factors in human life." With a symbolic action such as this where one would expect Philo to wax eloquent, he is rather unsure. While the action is definitely called a sign, Philo cannot find an application because of the change he has brought about in the meaning of the term. C. H. Dodd has also shown that the cognate verb σημαίνω may be used as a synonym for σημεῖον.[17] He brings the example where σημεῖον is contrasted with δῆλον, which carries the literal meaning (*De congressu* 155). In *De congressu* 172, it also carries this meaning, and is combined with ὑπονοίων: "Let us not, then, be misled by the actual words, but look at the meaning [σημαινόμενα] that lies beneath them." In contrast, sometimes the literal meaning is present (*De cheribim* 129, *De plantatione* 152, *De vita Mosis* 11:39). The most surprising thing about both usages is that neither is very prevalent, considering Philo's reputation as an allegorist. We note only eleven times where the word was used without its Stoic connotations.

Philo's philosophy is thus molded into his work, and it colors the usage of σημεῖον so that one cannot separate the two words when σημεῖον is used symbolically. The Platonic ideal world provides the basis for the allegorization. Thus, Philo finds himself out of his element when he comes to an Old Testament symbolic action, such as the sign of the binding of the law. We therefore find little in Philo that would lead us to see his use of the sign as the basic background for the Johannine usage.

THE JOHANNINE USE OF Σημεῖον

After this journey through the possible backgrounds for the Johannine usage of the sign, we turn to the use of the word itself in the Gospel of John. In comparison with the Synoptics, John has related the miracles of Jesus with an emphasis upon the meaning of the miracle rather than just the miracle itself.[18] Thus we have the right to expect that these signs were specifically chosen not only because they were miraculous but also because they carried meaning for the ministry of Jesus.

Fourteen of the seventeen times σημεῖον appears with ποιεῖν, nine times with πιστεύειν, and six times with verbs of seeing. The ideal pattern of the sign is that of an action (ποιεῖν) that is seen, which then produces faith. The action must reveal the work of Christ to the believer and have special meaning that increases faith. When the observer does not have faith, the sign places him in a position where he or she must decide either for or against the Christ.[19]

We shall first note those events in the Gospel which the author expressly calls signs. Then we shall proceed to note what might be common

17. Dodd, *Interpretation*, 141.
18. Mollat, "La Sèmeion Johannique," 210.
19. Deut 13:1–5; 18:1–5.

to them. Finally, we shall look at those events that are not so named to determine if we should consider them signs also.

A. There are five events in the Gospel which are called a σημεῖον: the miracle at the wedding in Cana (John 2:1–11), the healing of the ruler's son (4:46–54), the multiplication of loaves (6:5–13), the healing of the man born blind (9:1–7), and the raising of Lazarus from the dead (11:38–44). In each of these cases, the word σημεῖον is used expressly with regard to the event (2:11; 4:54; 5:14; 9:16; and 12:18 respectively).

B. The author considers all of the signs miraculous; thus, we will not debate whether the events were miraculous in light of our modern standards. The author and the people involved considered them miraculous, and thus were forced into a position of decision in regard to the person of Jesus.[20]

C. The signs call men and women to make decisions related to their faith in Jesus Christ, and in connection with every event called a sign, with the exception of the multiplication of bread (2:11; 4:53; 9:38; and 11:45, 48), all state an explicit connection between the signs and the faith they produced. After seeing the multiplication of bread, the people rightly interpret the event that had happened as a sign and say, "Surely this is the Prophet who is to come into the world" (6:14), which indicates an imperfect faith resulting from the sign. Such an imperfect faith is also present originally when the blind man of chapter 9 feels that Jesus is a prophet (9:17). He expresses his faith in terms of what Jesus can do (δύναται ποιεῖν; cf. also 3:2). Thus, we see the Jews' tendency to equate the ability to perform miracles with the divine authentication the prophet was supposed to present.[21]

In this emphasis on πιστεύειν, we see a clear parallel with the signs that Moses presented to the children of Israel (Exod 4:1, 5, 8–9). However, as with Moses in the Exodus (Num 14:11), Jesus has a consciousness that the faith produced by the signs is not a perfect faith, but one that must be nurtured unto perfection. The continued renewal in the disciples (John 2:11; 11:15; 20:8, 29, 31) and the growth of the blind man's faith show this sort of development. The desire of Jesus not to commit himself to those who had believed in him shows that he knew the quality of their signs-faith (2:23–25), and that he desired something more.

Not only does John indicate that this pattern involves his own interpretation of the events, but he also states that Jesus did signs with the

20. Wiles, *Spiritual Gospel*, 41.

21. Müller, *Das Heilsgeschehen*, 31.

significance of the events in mind. Jesus rejoices because the death of Lazarus (and the sign which results from it; 11:15) will bring the disciples into greater faith. Jesus prays openly to the Father that the multitude might come to believe "that the Father has sent him" through the sign which he is about to perform (11:42).

D. A word of revelation is connected with four of the five signs, often associated with the δόξα of God. We find such statements in 2:11: "He thus revealed his glory, and his disciples put their faith in him" and 11:4: "When he heard this, Jesus said, 'This sickness will not end in death. No, it is for God's glory so that God's Son might be glorified through it.'" Jesus thus conveys the divine agency of his mission in the revelation of his glory.

We can also trace the relation between the sign and the glory of God in the Old Testament (chiefly Num 14:22 and Isa 66:19) and in the writings of Qumran. The Johannine usage is thus not new, and the signs are meant to manifest the glory of God revealed in Jesus as the Christ. This glory can be no other than the divine presence as it is found through the Old Testament *kabod*—revealed in the true person of Jesus Christ as he works the works of his Father.

Through his use of the word λόγος, John is able to unite the Old Testament concept of the sign, which authenticates the word of the Lord, producing a unique element of self-revelation. In the Old Testament, the word came to the prophet, and the accompanying sign authenticated it. In the Gospel of John, the word came to Jesus, and the signs authenticated him. Thus, the authentication becomes a part of the revelation and bears witness to the mission of the Word. The glory of God is uniquely revealed in him and his work because he is God.[22]

For this reason, the discourses that accompany the signs invariably end with emphasis upon Jesus himself. The signs naturally lead to a position where one must decide whether the signs of Jesus authenticate the claims he makes about the work he does. We must agree with Karl Ludwig Schmidt, that Jesus both gives and is the sign.[23]

Only those who came to faith saw the glory of God in this as a sign.[24] Those who did not believe were placed in a position of crisis. After the healing of the blind man in John 9, the Pharisees are placed in a position where

22. Mussner, *Historical Jesus*, 20; Hofbeck, *Semeion*, 181; Bultmann, *Das Evangelium*, 33; Dibelius, *Die Formgeschichte*, 91.

23. Schmidt, "Der Johanneishce Charakter," 39–40.

24. Schmidt, "Der Johanneishce Charakter," 37.

they must decide either for or against Jesus. Their negative response forces them to take action against those who respond positively to him. After the raising of Lazarus, the same negative response is recorded as a result of the notable miracle. The hardness of heart that Pharaoh exhibited is now found in those who did not believe in the Christ.

This same self-revelation also occurs in the "I am" passages. Three of these themes (6:35, 48, 51; 8:12; 11:25) are related to the signs we are considering and speak of the self-revelation of the Christ. The healing of the nobleman's son is without such a word. We cannot say why, unless it might be that John saw no need for such a word when the man came to faith. In 2:11, the revelatory word comes only as an addition from the author following the account of the miracle.

E. When we turn to the relation of the discourses to the signs, we are dealing with a phenomenon that relates to only three of the five events that are called signs. In two of these three cases, the discourse comes before the sign, and in the third the discourse follows it. There is no discourse with the changing of the water to wine, or with the healing of the ruler's son. Perhaps the author feels there is no discourse necessary for these signs. The number involved is small in both cases—only the disciples in the first case, and only the ruler in the second. Both audiences immediately come to faith, so there is no explanation necessary.

In the latter two cases (John 9 and 11) where there is a discourse, it comes before the sign or during the narrative of it. Jesus makes a definite attempt with these discourses to explain what he will do. John 9:5 shows a definite relation between 8:12 and the miracle that follows: "While I am in the world, I am the Light of the world." The ταῦτα εἰπὼν at the beginning of 9:6 emphasizes this connection. The relation between the dialogue with Martha and the events that follow is also unmistakable.

As a result, we are only left with chapter 6, where the long dialogue-type discourse follows the sign and gives the sign its meaning. The point of the discourse is to correct a materialistic view of messianic salvation. The people must see not only the miracle involved, but they also must grasp the true meaning of the sign. When the people misunderstand the messianic gift of salvation, Jesus carefully instructs them that he is the one they seek, but the life he offers is different from what they had envisioned. When they do not accept the new offer, they depart.

These five marks of the sign should be considered when we return to the other events that may be signs in John's Gospel. As we have been able to note exceptions, we should not expect the other events examined to follow in all five points.

An example of such an event is the healing at the pool in Bethesda (5:2–9). While the healing is not called a σημεῖον (only ἔργον in verse 20), we can see how thoroughly the presentation by the evangelist fits the pattern of his other signs, as well. The author considers it miraculous, and Jesus openly proceeds to connect the event with a call to belief (v. 24). This aspect of revelation is expressed as strongly as with any of the signs: "καὶ πατέρα ἴδιον ἔλεγεν τὸν θεὸν ἴσον ἑαυτὸν ποιῶν τῷ θεῷ" (v. 18). This verse expresses the meaning of the glory of Christ and the understanding that, by the sign and the discourse, Jesus made himself equal with God (ἴσον ἑαυτὸν ποιῶν τῷ θεῷ). The concept of glory is involved again in verses 41 and 44, although more negatively than positively. The emphasis is placed on the inability to perceive the works of Jesus as divine authentication to the authority he claims. The discourse that follows the healing is in the form of a dialogue (vv. 17–47). It serves as an attempt to explain the significance of Jesus' action.

Even though this event is only called ἔργον, it is probably wise to consider it as a sign. There is thus a distinct relation between the ἔργα of Jesus and his σημεῖα. A work may take on a revelatory character and fill the role of a sign, but without such an interpretation supplied by the evangelist, we question the propriety of making a transition from ἔργον to σημεῖον too easily.

Such is the case with the miracle of the walking on the sea (6:17–21). While there is little doubt that the author considered the event miraculous, we find little indication that he considered it a sign. Rather, we fail to find those elements that delineate it as a Johannine sign. The result of the event is neither belief nor unbelief. Rather, they simply "came to land" (6:21). No revelatory word comes with the action. The action demonstrates (not symbolizes) the superiority of the Lord over nature, but there is no emphasis on this in the text. Neither is there a descriptive discourse. Thus, while the event is undoubtedly miraculous to the author, he makes no indication that he considered it a sign.[25]

The cleansing of the temple (2:11–22) presents a more difficult problem. The event was not miraculous, and yet the Old Testament and classical background for the sign has not made this mandatory. We merely note this

25. Bernard, *Critical and Exegetical Commentary*, 1:xc; Schmidt, "Der Johanneishce Charakter," 39.

as a Johannine characteristic of the sign. However, other indications of the sign are also missing, particularly the revelatory word and the placement of the hearer in a position of decision with regard to the Christ. The action rather calls forth the demand for a sign. The emphasis on believing is not found. Rather, the element of belief comes only after the resurrection is actualized (v. 22).

John presents the Jews as understanding this as a prophetic action, and thus they seek a sign to authenticate it. This follows the pattern of the Old Testament. Jesus responds with a word that the disciples interpret to refer to the destruction of the body of Jesus (v. 19), and thus to refer to the resurrection as the authentication Jesus offered as a sign.

Dodd sees the demand for a sign (v. 18) parallel to 6:26, where the Jews demand another sign after the feeding of the multitude.[26] But this comparison falls short in several ways. Not only is the temple cleansing not called a sign, but in the miraculous feeding Jesus directs the hearers to the sign that has already been done, rather than a future event. The discourse calls attention to no further sign, but it points to Jesus as the bread of life. In the temple cleansing, however, Jesus points to a future sign which will authenticate his action and the divine nature to be revealed most fully in his resurrection from the dead. While the use of σημεῖον characteristically refers to a miraculous deed, Dodd suggests that the evangelist considered such actions as the cleansing of the temple to be signs. It is possible that he did, however, and that the Jews did not (2:18). The fact that the cleansing of the temple is followed by 2:23, which mentions that Jesus did many signs in Jerusalem, does not really prove that the cleansing is a sign.[27] It must be considered a prophetic action, which called forth the need of a sign to authenticate it.

The final event about which there is serious debate is the resurrection of Jesus. The crowning event of his earthly life differs from the other signs because there is disagreement as to whether it is called a σημεῖον. Mollat puts forth three indications that John considers the whole passion a sign.[28] First, he cites the passage where Jesus spoke regarding the destruction of the Jewish temple when asked for a sign. The disciples later came to understand this saying in regard to the resurrection (2:18–22). Second, he refers to the use of σημαίνω referring to the crucifixion of Jesus (12:33; 18:32).

26. Dodd, *Interpretation*, 301.

27. Brown, *Gospel According to John (i–xii)*, 528.

28. Mollat, "La Sèmeion Johannique," 209–10.

Third, the reference to "many other signs and wonders" in 20:30 implies the event just completed—the resurrection—was considered a sign.[29]

Of these arguments, the second seems the weakest. While the Philonic usage of σημαίνω is a synonym for σημεῖον, it may also be translated "to indicate." John uses this sense in 21:19 referring to the death of Peter. Σημαίνω signifies something which will happen in future time. It does not set aside the event as a sign. Of the remaining two arguments, the latter seems stronger than the former, but both seem valid, especially in light of their agreement.

The resurrection does differ distinctly from the other signs in one aspect: there is no record of the actual event. Rather, we have four scenes in chapter 20, where people discover the empty tomb and/or come face to face with the risen Lord. In each of these resurrection stories, the affirmation of belief is evident. In 20:8, the two disciples "see and believe," verse 18 pictures Mary seeing and proclaiming newfound faith, verse 20 pictures the rejoicing at the sight of the risen Lord, and verse 28 shows Thomas confessing his faith with the strongest confession in the entire Gospel. Finally, the emphasis on believing as the result of seeing the sign is strengthened by the blessing of those who believe without having seen (20:29).

The words of revelation noted in the earlier miracles are not here. In their place, we find Jesus revealing himself,[30] but this also might be expected in John, for Jesus is the Word, and the revelation of the risen body is that which makes the sign most meaningful for those who see and come to believe. The confession of Thomas is the highest expression of divinity found in the Gospel. The four events take the place of the discourses, for they make clear the meaning of the sign.[31]

Thus, seven signs are found in the Gospel. The first two are in Cana of Galilee (John 2 and 4) and result in belief. The second two (John 5 and 6) have a teaching calling the hearers to deepen their faith through dialogue-type discourses. The third pair (John 9 and 11) have negative effects on the Jewish leaders, who find out about them through informers. Both have related discourses before the actual miracle is performed. The final sign (John 11) prefigures the resurrection as the crowning event of the Gospel. The supreme revelation in Jesus Christ produces the perfect and complete

---

29. Martyn, *History and Theology*, 81–82.

30. Hofbeck, *Semeion*, 86.

31. Bultmann, *Theologie des Neuen Testaments*, 409.

faith that God requires. It stands by itself to complete the pattern of the sign in the Gospel of John.

IMPLICATIONS OF THE JOHANNINE SIGN

One cannot consider what a sign is without also turning to consider the significance for the author. While it is impossible for us, in a work of this size, to consider separately the significance of each miracle, we should consider certain key questions.

First, we must face the relation of the sign to the historical. Does the interpretation of an event as a sign have any effect upon the reliability of the historicity of the events involved? Or does the author fabricate the events to fill one's need in the signifying message he proclaims?

We have no precedent that such events ever existed in purely symbolic form, or that historical events were created through the quest for a symbolic meaning.[32] When Paul allegorizes the story of Sarah and Hagar, he does not suggest that the historical element of the story was nonexistent (Gal 4:21–31). The same would be true for the symbolic interrelation of the crossing of the Red Sea (1 Cor 10:1–11) and Peter's interpretation of the ark (1 Pet 3:20–21). The figurative interpretation does not imply that the historic event was nonexistent. Rather, the historic event produces a milieu from which the figure can be drawn.

We are forced to take note of stark realism in the life of Jesus as John presents it. This is a flesh-and-blood account.[33] Hoskyns emphasizes that the setting of the Gospel is in real life.[34] Apart from the life and death of Jesus, no understanding of the Gospel is possible. John cannot be accused on comparative grounds of fabricating a history, for he makes no more from the history than the Synoptics do. Rather, he places emphasis on the life of Jesus and the faith that it demands in the human situation.[35]

On several occasions, we may note that the interpretation of an event given in the Gospel is dependent on the historical occurrence. The discourse of the bread of life (John 6) especially is built upon the actual happening

---

32. Barrett, *Gospel*, 17.

33. Mollat and Braun, *L'Évangile*.

34. Hoskyns, *Fourth Gospel*, 117.

35. Schmidt, "Der Johanneishce Charakter," 41–42.

that came before it. But in all these signs, the meaning of the event for the life of Christ is dependent on the historical accuracy of John's account.[36]

C. K. Barrett has also noted this relationship between the signs and the historical in John 9 and 11.[37] Such an interrelatedness requires that the sign cannot have meaning without the happening of the historical event. The miracle is the basis for the meaning of the sign, and without the event there can be no interpretation.

Just as important for the Johannine account, though, is the relation of the interpretation to the historical. In the Synoptics, one is allowed to consider the miracles of healing as acts of benevolence—manifestations of the power of God to alleviate suffering. John does not permit this. Signs must be interpreted as actions meant to call persons to faith and to reveal the nature of the Messiah.[38] For the sign to be a sign, the interpretation must be present. It must be more than an event. As we saw from the Old Testament background, both are such a unity that there can be no separation.

John is able to consider the signs of Jesus as a part of the witness of Christ, so the close relation between sign and witness cannot be missed. We have noted that the ἔργον in chapter 5 should properly be considered a sign. The miracle authenticates the meaning of Jesus' statement in verse 36b: "For the very work [ἔργα] that the Father has given me to finish, and which I am doing, testifies that the Father has sent me." It shows an important relation between the signs and their witness to Jesus.[39] Without the proper interpretation, the ἔργον remains merely a work. But with it, the work becomes a witness to Jesus Christ as the coming Messiah, thereby becoming a sign.

In light, especially, of Jewish eschatological and messianic expectation in Jesus' day, we would be negligent to overlook the eschatological aspect of the sign.[40] One of the functions the sign developed in later writings was in regard to the apocalyptic. In this way, the sign was expected to answer the question, "When?" The Jews came to expect that the Messiah would bring signs when he came,[41] and in a real way, the signs became eschatological actions. They signified the end of the age and the coming of the final time.

36. Haenchen, "Das Johannesevangelium," 889.

37. Barrett, *Gospel*, 17.

38. Cullmann, *Heil als Geschichte*, 250.

39. Charlier, "La Notion," 439.

40. Hofbeck, *Semeion*, 161.

41. John 7:31; Strack-Billerbeck, "Dreizigster Exkurs," 977–1015.

Jesus' word regarding the destruction of the temple (John 2:11) signaled the end of that age.[42]

This messianic expectation probably stemmed from Isaiah 35:5–6:

> Then the eyes of the blind shall be opened,
> and the ears of the deaf unstopped;
> then shall the lame man leap like a deer,
> and the tongue of the dumb shout for joy.

The messianic time must manifest itself with regard to the actions. In this light, there are many parallels between the Johannine sign and the σημεῖα καὶ τέρατα of the Exodus period. These Old Testament wonders were peculiar in that they signaled the beginning of a new age. Thus we note the conscious reference to the works of Jesus as σημεῖα καὶ τέρατα (4:48; 20:30). In chapter 6, when the people demand another sign, they seek a continuation of the miracle of the feeding of the nation in the wilderness, following the pattern from Exodus (6:31). Jeremias notes the particularly strong expectation for the Mosaic pattern in the time of Christ.[43] The Exodus period should be the pattern for the messianic time in the Jewish mind. The origin of the messianic movements in the desert forms a part of this pattern and points to the period of the foundation of the Jewish nation.

Thus, we can expect an anticipatory nature as a part of the sign, as signs created expectation in the minds of those who saw them.[44] They pointed to the coming of the new age. By their breaking into history, they introduced the new age, the last days.

The signs of Jesus thus point us to John's understanding of messianic salvation, which is interpreted through the person of the Christ in his performance of signs. An important eschatological function of the sign is to establish the messianic authority of the Christ and to challenge mistaken contemporary Jewish understandings of messianic salvation. The latter becomes particularly clear in the discourse on the bread of life, but that clarity should not limit this function to the signs of Jesus. Indeed, all of the actions of Jesus pictured in the Gospel of John bring the message of its new vision salvation into clearer focus.

The question of whether the signs of John should be symbolically interpreted is one that requires closer scholarly attention. Many promote

---

42. McCool, *Introduction*, 113–14.

43. Jeremias, "Μωϋσῆς," 864, 877.

44. Haenchen, "Der Vater," 209.

such an interpretation; yet, as one inspects their work, one finds a great deal of fuzziness, especially about the meaning of the term "symbolic." The need for clarification in the use of this term is evident. Does an author's use of the term "symbolic" mean a quest for images that convey hidden truth? Is it a quest for quirks of style that are meant to be repositories of hidden truth? Is it an exploration of figures of speech that the author uses? Is it a quest for a deeper spiritual meaning behind the actions of Jesus that the author intended to portray? In referring to "symbolic meaning," is the modern author really considering what John intended as theological significance? All of these questions must be answered before we can grasp what a "scholarly" work means when it says "symbolic."

Symbolism within the Gospel of John must thus be approached with extreme caution.[45] Not only is there very little agreement as to what should be considered symbolism, but there are also many other good reasons why the search for the symbolic interpretation of a passage poses a challenge to the exegete. First, we have no precedent in this genre of literature for the hidden symbolic interpretation of a text, as Bernard notes:

> It is now to be observed that none of the early masters of the allegorical method, whether Jewish or Christian, invented an incident or constructed a number in order to teach a spiritual lesson. . . . The fables of Aesop were, frankly, constructed to convey moral lessons. Our Lord gave to this method the sanction of His own authority, for He habitually taught by parables, "earthly stories with heavenly meaning"; and His example has been followed by Christian teachers in every age, from the *Shepherd of Hermas* in the second century to the *Pilgrim's Progress* in the seventeenth. But the allegorical *interpreter* and the *author* of parables follow distinct paths, and are not to be confused, the one with the other.[46]

Even Philo, Clement, and Origen, who followed the symbolic approach, did not interpret their own works symbolically. One must face the problems of the symbolic in John because he calls our attention to the fact that he uses an interpretative element. Paul also uses allegory and typology, but this does not cause us to search to find such figures where the author does not call our attention to them.

---

45. Hooke, *Alpha and Omega*, 275, in which he calls C. K. Barrett extremely cautious in his approach to the symbolism of the Gospel of John. We believe that there is much merit in the approach taken by Barrett.

46. Bernard, *St. John*, 1:lxxxv; emphasis original.

Second, John does not write from the milieu of Platonic philosophy. It is no accident of history that the first Christian writers who followed Philo were Alexandrians: Clement and Origen. Much of what they did was done on their acceptance of the philosophy Philo accepted. The earliest patristic Christian writers did not use the philosophy of their day as a background for their writings. It is only after Justin and Tatian that such philosophical thought affected early Christian thought and writing. The presupposition of extensive symbolic interpretation in the Gospel of John is not possible without Plato.

Third, we may note a sharp contrast between the writings of Philo and the Gospel of John with regard to their use of names. Symbolism becomes one of the most important parts of the Philonic process of allegorization. Names carry a chief source of symbolic meaning, and are important where σημεῖον and σύμβολον appear together in Philo. How different this is in the Gospel of John. John also displays a consciousness for names, but this consciousness is rather involved with the fact that his Greek readers do not understand the Hebrew names he is using. Thus, in John we often find notations added to names that do not connote symbolic meaning, but are simply translations.

Fourth, there is a sharp difference between the Johannine use of the word σημαίνω and its usage in Philo. In the latter, this term may be used to point to an allegorical meaning, although this is not always the case. By way of contrast in John, it points to some event in the future, which is being foretold.

Fifth, in the Old Testament the sign and the symbolic action were by no means synonymous. Many symbolic actions were not considered signs. Many signs, such as the stopping of the sun's movement or the sign of the young woman's son in Isaiah, cannot be construed as symbolic actions of the prophets. Nothing would cause the people to wonder about their meaning as with the Greek sign. Rather they were quite explicit. The meaning of these signifying actions is set forth with the prophet's action so that the people observing them might understand the meaning of what the prophet was doing.

This seems to be the pattern followed in John. We must grasp the symbolic in John, as it is related to the sign. John shows us that the interpretive is present. However, we cannot just assume that this element is present when the text does not show us that it is. The pattern of the Old Testament causes us to question the propriety of extending the symbolic meaning to all and searching in order that we might find it.

Finally, certain things that many have considered symbolic in nature have been shown to have proper historical settings as plausible events. A good example is found in the work of Jeremias dealing with the geographical details of the pool of Bethesda.[47] Details, formerly considered by many to be symbolic, have now been shown simply to fit a geographical setting. This, of course, causes us to question the propriety of the remaining symbolic interpretations.

In the Johannine context, there are seven signs that we have considered. The fourth, fifth, and sixth of these are bound together with "I am" metaphors, so they must be interpreted alongside the meaning given by the evangelist. The third sign (John 5) has a long explanatory discourse, which shows Jesus to be the Lord of the Sabbath. But from there on, the meaning of a sign becomes less clear. We must rely on the presence of water pots for the Jewish purification to be the key, pointing to the fact that the new purification is superior to the old. With the healing of the ruler's son, there is so little that can be interpreted symbolically that even C. H. Dodd contributes only two paragraphs in dealing with it. He joins it within the second episode with John 5 and the sign of the healing at Bethesda,[48] yet he also links the healing to the first sign because both took place in Cana of Galilee. Such paucity of material for what the evangelist called a sign should cause us to be cautious with our applications of symbolic interpretations.

However, the seventh sign—the resurrection—presents the chief problem. Of what is it a symbol? Yet, when we accept the resurrection as a sign, we should make it the chief sign. The sermons of Acts consider it the chief legitimation of the fact that Jesus was what he claimed to be. The resurrection of Lazarus shows Jesus fulfilling the claims that he had made in the Gospel of John in such a way that it brought forth faith, which became the basis for the church. But it does not symbolize the restoration of life; it is the restoration of life. It reveals Jesus to be the Christ in the fullness of his divine essence, as demonstrated by his signs.

47. Jeremias, *Rediscovery of Bethesda*.
48. Dodd, *Interpretation*, 318–19.

CONCLUSIONS

John has shown us seven signs that authenticate the person and mission of Jesus. This element of authentication places members of the audience in a position wherein they must decide whether Jesus is or is not the Christ. The author is careful to locate each event in an explicit place in history, so the signs thus become eschatological events illuminating the meaning of the messianic salvation. We must, however, approach their semeiological function and significance with caution. We should not make the mistake of concluding that a sign must be a symbolic action only. The two concepts are separate in the Old Testament, although they are also joined together on occasions.

Above all, we can see in the Johannine signs of Jesus the union of the Old Testament aspects of the prophetic word and its authentication. The supreme manifestation of the prophet's divine commission is the declarative "Word." The prophet's signs then give authentication and meaning to the divine agent and his message. Likewise, in the Gospel of John, Jesus performs signs, and he is that which he signifies.

CHAPTER 3

DOUBLE MEANING IN THE FOURTH GOSPEL

The prophet Amos has left us with a polished address. At one point, he chides "those who rejoice in the conquest of Lo-Debar" and "those who say, 'Have we not taken for ourselves Karnaim with our own strength?'" (Amos 6:13). Cohen has shown us that the implication here is to two border towns that were taken during the expansion of Jeroboam II.[1] These towns were fortresses in the border area between Gilead and Syria. Their names carried meaning that provided the import of the prophet's message. *Lo-Debar* means "nothing," or "a thing of no worth." *Karnaim* means "horns." When these cities were taken, there were those who boasted that their capture was a mark of national strength. Now, with the return of Syria to power and the relative weakening of their Assyrian adversary, these two former prizes had become the scene of a very unpopular defensive border war between Israel and Syria.

Thus, Amos is pointing to the double meaning of the names of these towns, leading readers to infer his message not only from the names, but also from the meaning of the names, of the towns. Those who had rejoiced at the capture of Lo-Debar were not now nearly so happy in that which many considered "nothing." That which had been considered horns of strength, the city of Karnaim, now was considered to be much more of a thorn in the nation's side, sapping its strength.

A literary device by the author of the Fourth Gospel follows this dual pattern. The author uses words with two meanings, both of which may be applicable. He probably did not intend to present an either/or situation wherein commentators and Christians must make a choice of one meaning. Rather, he employs a distinctive device, where both meanings of the word apply.

1. Cohen, "Political Background," 153–60.

We shall begin from here to explore the alleged double meanings in the Gospel of John to see the author's pattern of use. We shall note: (1) the double meanings based on the Greek alone; (2) the double meanings based on both the Greek and the Aramaic, or Hebrew terminology behind it; (3) the possible double meaning that is derived from an Aramaic double meaning which does not come into the Greek text; (4) the double meaning of words used in a pericope or parable-like saying; (5) the double meaning of verbs based on the ambiguity of mode; and (6) the words which rely on a figurative meaning for the fuller expression of the meaning of the evangelist.

DOUBLE MEANING ON THE BASIS
OF THE GREEK WORDS ALONE

A good place to start our exploration of the double meanings in the Gospel of John is with the word "ἄνωθεν" as it is used in John 3:3. The alternative meanings are very clear and very much debated. According to Bauer, ἄνωθεν may have three meanings. Only number 1 ("from above") and number 3 ("again, anew") interest us.

One group of commentators claims the word can only mean "again or anew." These commentators[2] follow the early Syriac (Peshito), Memphitic, Aethiopic, and the Latin versions, including the Vulgate, which translate with *denuo* and words related to it.[3] The English versions of the Bible generally follow this pattern. The major exceptions to this are the Great Bible (Coverdale, changed from the earlier Coverdale Bible) and the Bishops Bible of 1572 (changed from the earlier rendering of 1568). Luther uses the translation "*von neuem*," also following this trend.

These commentators may point to Galatians 4:9, where ἄνωθεν is used by Paul to mean "again." They may also point to Justin, who gives us one of our earliest patristic citations of this verse, substituting ἀναγεννάω for the more ambiguous term chosen by John,[4] a term used by Peter to express the entrance into the new life (1 Pet 1:3, 23).

Another group of commentators claim that the word ἄνωθεν can only mean "from above." These commentators[5] may point to the Aramaic

2. Zahn, *Das Evangelium des Johannes*, 183–84; Bultmann, *Das Evangelium*, 95n2.

3. Westcott, *Gospel*, 63.

4. Martyr, *First Apology*, I.61.

5. Schnackenburg, *Das Johannesevangelium*, 1; Mollat and Braun, *L'Évangile*; Büchsel,

word that probably lies behind it. It is not capable of meaning other than "from above." Such an argument always seems tenuous, because it involves a postulation of a term as an antecedent. In addition to our inability to obtain surety as to the Aramaic original (if there was one), the self-evident truth that the talk with Nicodemus was not recorded on the spot, but rather recorded as remembered at a later date, make such arguments tentative. The evangelist emphasizes that the birth mentioned is a spiritual birth with divine origin. The Greek writers from Origen onward generally use this translation. In addition, there are the translations of the Harclean Syriac, Armenian, and Gothic versions, not to mention the Zürcher Bible, which uses "*von oben herab.*"

The context of John provides other uses of the word, all of which are translated "from above." In 3:31 and 19:11, the reference is to divine origin. In 19:23, the reference is to the continuous weave in Jesus' robe "from the top" throughout.

The third group of commentators follows the course suggested by Bauer in his lexicon: "3. *again, anew* . . . ἀ. γεννηθῆναι is purposely ambiguous and means both *born from above* and *born again* J. 3:3, 7."[6] In this latter group we find C. K. Barrett,[7] Cullmann,[8] Hunter,[9] and Tasker.[10] C. K. Barrett says, "ἄνωθεν is capable of two meanings and here it probably has both. It may mean 'from above' but also 'afresh, again.' The birth which is required is certainly a second birth, but it is not (see v. 4) a mere repetition of man's first birth, but a begetting from above from God."[11] Bauer shows the same with his emphasis on "Zeugung durch Gott" and the connection with the Pauline phrase καινὴ κτίσις.[12] Thus ἄνωθεν indicates not only what may be visibly happening, a birth in water, but also what happens unseen, a birth from above through the Holy Spirit. We might compare this with the sign, which not only related to us an event, but also led us to the divine meaning of that event.

Das Evangelium.

6. Bauer, *Greek-English Lexicon*, at place; emphasis original.

7. Barrett, *Gospel*, 173–74.

8. Cullmann, "Der Johanneische Gebrauch," 364–65.

9. Hunter, *Gospel*, 38.

10. Tasker, *Gospel*, 70.

11. Barrett, *Gospel*, 171–72.

12. Bauer, *Das Johannesevangelium*, 48–49.

We are not dealing with figurative speech, but concrete meanings of the word. The double meaning is thus not a metaphor or a simile. The author's deliberate choice involves the dual aspects of a word and intimates the correctness of both.[13]

Another text we might place in the above category is 11:24, where ἀνίστημι is used both to refer to the resurrection of Lazarus and to the faith of the Christian in the resurrection on the last day. Martha's response shows that she understands Jesus' words with regard to the last day. Jesus does not attempt to say she is wrong, but shows her that her understanding is not complete. Not only will her brother rise in the last day (as will all believers), but he will also live again now through his miraculous resurrection. The events of the remainder of the chapter show the fulfillment of the double meaning.[14]

The double meaning of βαστάζω (12:6) is without a Hebrew background, although there is rich evidence in the Koine Greek for its dual use.[15] Βαστάζω means not only "to carry," but also "to pilfer" or "to steal." The implication is not only that Judas was the treasurer of the group, but also that he was a thief. He was lifting the funds. In modern terminology, he was embezzling. The evangelist thus emphasizes the double meaning by stating κλέπτης ἦν.[16]

In 14:2, a spiritual meaning forms the basis for the double meaning of the noun, μοναί.[17] Μοναί refers not only to the dwelling places we can expect with God, but also that we can look forward to dwelling with Christ spiritually.

With regard to the double meaning of εἰς τέλος (John 13:1), Bauer points out that this usage may mean both to the very end or to the greatest extent."[18] John intended not only to show that Jesus loved his disciples to the end of his life, but also in the highest manner.

In the same verse, there is a possible reference to the *agape* feast of the early Christians, which Jesus would have just completed with his disciples. Bo Reicke points out that in John 13:1, there is a textual variant to ἠγάπησεν, which may refer to the meal just eaten, a possible reference to

---

13. Bultmann, *Das Evangelium*, 95.

14. Cullmann, "Der Johanneische Gebrauch," 369.

15. Deissmann, *Neue Bibelstudien*, 85; Moulton and Milligan, *Vocabulary*.

16. Hoskyns, *Fourth Gospel*, 415; Hunter, *Gospel*, 121.

17. Gundry, "In My Father's House," 68–72.

18. Bauer, *Das Johannesevangelium*, 167.

the sacramental meal that Christians came to call *agape*.[19] This connection is made particularly clear when we see καὶ δείπνου γινομένου, "and having finished the meal." Thus, the word ἀγαπάω should be seen in both of its emphases. The love Jesus had for his disciples is evident here and through the remainder of the farewell discourse. The meal that they just concluded was a special symbol of that love, a symbol that carried over into the Christian church, under the name of a love feast, the *agape*. This reference to the love of Jesus probably shows the connection between Jesus' love for his disciples and the origin of the feast.

The word from the cross, τετέλεσται, "it is finished" (19:30) gives us another double meaning.[20] "It is finished" not only applies to the chronological end of Jesus' life on earth, but also to the theological goal of the mission for which he came.[21] Both are completed in this one act. Both are expressed in this one word.

We may add the few instances in the Gospel where the double meaning does not come from the intrinsic meaning of the words, but is involved with the churchly understanding of the words. The interrelation between the double meaning, the literary standpoint, and irony becomes very evident, at least at one point. In 11:50, the evangelist records the words of the high priest, Caiaphas: "You do not realize that it is better for you that one man die for the people than that the whole nation perish." To this the evangelist adds that the high priest had spoken by prophecy without understanding it. Then he clarifies the prophecy with the full meaning of his words. "Jesus would die for the Jewish nation [ἔθνος], and not only for that nation but also for the scattered children of God, to bring them together and make them one" (vv. 51b–52). Thus, John draws upon the double meaning of the word "ἔθνος," which may mean the Jewish nation, or it may extend the divine blessing to potential believers in the diaspora.

In 2:19 we find this: "Destroy this temple and in three days I will raise it again." While the evangelist says that this refers to the crucifixion and resurrection of the Christ, commentators who see in this the destruction of the temple by the Jewish nation are probably right. Λύσατε, the second person plural, calls attention to the role of the Jews in the matter. The Jews' revolt against Rome led to the destruction of the temple. There was tradition that the coming of the Messiah would bring the destruction of the

19. Reicke, *Diakonie, Festfreude und Zelos*, 352–53.

20. Cullmann, "Der Johanneische Gebrauch," 370.

21. Dodd, *Historical Tradition*, 124.

Jewish temple.[22] The early church considered themselves a part of the risen body of the Christ, the church, which replaced the temple of the Jewish nation.[23]

> It presupposes the equivalence of the 'body' of Christ with the Church which is the spiritual 'temple,' and we have reason to believe that this double equivalence goes back to Paul. Yet the association of the Cleansing of the Temple with the death and resurrection of Jesus (in some sense) seems to be given in the tradition as known to John; for (i) the testimony of Ps lxviii. 10 is an oblique pointer to the approaching death of Jesus, implying that his action in the temple sealed his doom—which is what we should gather from Mark; and (ii) the 'three days' interval of the temple-saying belongs essentially to the tradition of the resurrection in all its forms.[24]

We shall comment further on this passage later.[25] C. K. Barrett notes a possible double meaning in the passage where the Holy Spirit is promised (16:13). Here the question arises as to the meaning of τὰ ἐρχόμενα. Does it refer to the theological explanation of the events of the passion that comes that night, or to the eschatological events that the evangelist himself was still awaiting? Barrett believed that the answer is both.[26]

DOUBLE MEANING ON THE BASIS OF SEMITIC AND GREEK WORDS

The word "ὑψόω" in the Gospel of John appears five times (twice in 3:14; 8:28; 12:32, 34), each time with connotations that lead us to the double meaning. It differs from those words considered above, in that there is a Hebrew equivalent which can form the basis for the double meaning. But it is important to note that this Hebrew equivalent is not necessary.

Ὑψόω is used fifteen times in the New Testament outside of the Gospel of John. In each case, it has connotations of exaltation. On the human level, it refers to the exaltation of a person or a town either in its own time or in

22. Schnackenburg, *Das Johannesevangelium*, 365.

23. Rom 12:3–4; Eph 1:23; 4:12; 5:30; and Col 3:15 refer to the church as the body of Christ. 1 Cor 3:16 and 6:19 show that the church referred to its members as the temple.

24. Dodd, *Historical Tradition*, 161.

25. Cf. pp. pp. 82–84.

26. Barrett, *Gospel*, 408.

the time to come (Matt 11:23; 23:12; Luke 1:52; 10:15; 14:11; 18:14; 2 Cor 11:7, Jas 4:10; Pet 5:6). In Acts 2:33 and 5:31, ὑψόω refers to the exaltation of Christ to the right hand of God after his ascension.

One cannot overlook the difference in the Johannine usage. After the prediction of the death in 12:32, John says that he used "being lifted up" to indicate the manner of death he would die. Then the people who have understood this correctly as a prediction of his death raise the question: is not the Messiah to abide forever? The only adequate understanding of the passage comes through the double meaning. His "lifting up" is also his exaltation to God.

We have a basis for this double meaning in the Hebrew equivalent. In Genesis 40:13 and 19, the dream interpretations of Joseph involve the "lifting up of the head" of the servants involved. In one case, this *nasa' ro'sch* involved the restoration of the servant to power, while in the other it involved the hanging of the servant. But these Scriptures cannot be used to demonstrate more than the double meaning of the Hebrew thought pattern behind the word ὑψόω, for in neither case does the LXX use ὑψόω to translate *nasa*.

Schlatter[27] has shown that there is a word, "'izd·qeph," which may mean both "to be lifted up" and "to crucify." He adds that this word was only prominently used for "crucified" in North Syria. In addition to this, Kittel shows that *ts l j b '*, from the root *ts l b* may mean "pfählen."[28]

They also show us the difficulty in postulating a Semitic word that was translated into the Greek. In most cases, there is more than one word available. Therefore, it is impossible for us to express accurately that which might have been the original language.

We may also see a rich background for the double meaning in Greek literature. Greek writers of this time used the root from which ὑψόω comes to refer to both the exaltation and crucifixion of persons.[29]

This provides the background upon which the evangelist has expressed his double meaning. In 3:14–15, we find the first usage of ὑψόω. "Just as Moses lifted up [ὑψόω] the snake in the wilderness, so the Son of Man must be lifted up [ὑψόω], that everyone who believes may have eternal

---

27. Schlatter, *Der Evangelist Johannes*, 96.

28. Kittel, "*iad`qeph*," 282–85.

29. Homer, *Batrachomyomachia*, 81; Artemidorus Daldianus, *Onircriticon*, I.76, II.53, IV.49.

life in him." The use of the Son of Man here and in each of the other passages shows the emphasis upon the glorification.

This mention of the crucifixion in the context of glorification places
John in a decidedly different perspective than we find in the other Gospels.
In the Synoptics, the crucifixion is the low point of Jesus' ministry, the dark
point, which the disciples did not understand. It caused their scattering.
In John, his post-resurrection point of view allows him to see the death of
Christ in a truer perspective. For John, the crucifixion becomes a part of
the process of the glorification of Jesus. In other New Testament references
to Christ, ὑψόω refers to his ascension. In John, the crucifixion is considered a part of this ascent. The process of the revelation of the "lifting up"
of Jesus is one that begins before his resurrection and ascension, and the
crucifixion forms a definite part of it.[30]

This process of glorification continues as the emphasis of John 17. It is
probably Isaiah 52:13 that provides the union of terms for the glorification
in the mind of John. Here we might translate the LXX: "See, my servant
will act wisely and he will be raised [ὑψωθήσεται] and lifted up and highly
exalted [δοξασθήσεται]." This passage shows the two terms for glorification
in parallel.[31] John has chosen to use ὑψόω not only to signify the glorification, but also the crucifixion of the Lord.

When we turn to 8:28, we may note the same double intent. "When
you have lifted up [ὑψώσητε] the Son of Man, then you will know that I am
the one I claim to be [ἐγώ εἰμι]." The emphasis on the crucifixion comes
through the use of the second person plural of the verb. The Jews could
hardly be said to exalt the Christ to heaven. Their action must refer to the
crucifixion.

However, by their action, they unknowingly cooperate in the fore-
ordained plan of God, as the glorification of the Son of Man takes place
through their misdeed.[32] It is appropriate that, in this passage, "Son of Man"
is joined with ἐγώ εἰμι, connoting its divine implications.[33] The cross will
be the complete manifestation of the obedience of Christ to the will of the
Father, and thus the revelation of his origin. Through the crucifixion, the
Jews should finally be able to see the glorification of the Son of Man and
know that Jesus is God's Son and their Lord.

30. Cullmann, "L'Évangile," 116.

31. Lindars, *New Testament Apologetics*, 136.

32. Brown, *Gospel According to John (i–xii)*, 384.

33. Barrett, *Gospel*, 284.

The last passage (12:32, 34) presents a slight change. The glorification is emphasized, but not so strongly. Jesus will draw all people to himself through his being "lifted up." On the other hand, the author makes special emphasis of the fact that Jesus spoke this to indicate the death he would die (12:34). This is further emphasized in 18:32, when the Jews deliver Jesus to the Romans for crucifixion: "This happened so that the words Jesus had spoken indicating the kind of death he was going to die might be fulfilled." When the Jews delivered Jesus to Pilate, his prediction was thus fulfilled by being "lifted up from the earth" in his death.

> The expression ὑψωθῶ ἐκ τῆς γῆς might, with perfect propriety, be applied to death by hanging or crucifixion, especially in view of the apparently widely known double entente that we have noticed. The death of Christ by crucifixion, the only method of execution which (along with other modes of hanging) can appropriately be described in the terms ὑψωθῶ ἐκ τῆς γῆς, is signifying the reality of Christ's crucifixion which is the beginning of his exaltation of the glory of Christ.[34]

This double entendre emphasizes once again the involvement with the historical. Thus, ὑψόω refers to a concrete historical event. It also emphasizes Jesus' glorification. John has chosen the double meaning of this work to combine perfectly the inseparableness of the event with its interpretation.[35]

This use of double meaning is separated distinctly from the allegorical. Both of the meanings of the word are actual and in common use. Both are readily applicable and not hidden, as we find with the allegory.[36]

The Hebrew background can also be observed in 3:16. The meaning of ἔδωκεν here is questionable. Does it refer to the incarnation in the sense of ἀποστέλλω, or does it refer to Calvary in the sense of παραδίδωμι? Verse 17 emphasizes the first, while verses 14 and 15, where the Son of Man is lifted up, point us to the latter.

The key to this double meaning is found in the Old Testament use of *natan*. References where *natan* means "to give" are numerous in the Old Testament. The key reference meaning "to give up to death" is Isaiah 53:12: "Therefore I will give him a portion among the great and he will divide

34. Dodd, *Interpretation*, 247.
35. Vergote, "L'Exaltation du Christ," 222.
36. Schnackenburg, *Das Johannesevangelium*, 181.

the spoils with the strong, because he poured out [παρεδόθη] his life unto death." In this passage, παρεδόθη is a translation of the Hebrew *natan*.[37]

In John 5:6, ὑγιὴς probably relates to the Hebrew word *shalom*. This word stands for completeness, soundness, welfare, or peace. It is used both for the soundness in physical body (Hezekiah's thanksgiving; Isa 18:17) and for peace in our relationship with God (Isa 53:5; 54:10). Both of these concepts are involved in Jesus' offer. He provides physical healing, but more than this he shows concern that the spiritual aspect of the cure also continues. "See, you are well again. Stop sinning or something worse may happen to you" (John 5:14). In 7:23, Jesus seems to refer to this sign as the healing of a "whole" man. The contrast with circumcision indicates that not only was the physical outward man healed, but also the inward man.[38]

The expression "living water" is used twice in John (4:10 and 7:39). The double meaning draws from the vernacular use of the term to mean "running water," as opposed to water that had to be drawn from a well, and from Jesus' implication that the woman will find the water that Jesus gives in the form of teaching that will produce eternal life within her (ὕδωρ ζῶν = *majim hajjim*, Gen 26:19; Lev 14:5; Jer 2:13; cf. Did 7:1–2).[39] While the woman originally thought of the running water, Jesus proceeded to direct her thoughts to the living water, which should give her life eternal.

We find the same figure used in 7:39, but in a small parable where both meanings are contained in the same words. (We shall discuss this aspect of double meaning more fully in a later section.) Here the figure is expressed as the person who would have running water flowing from him (a quite imaginary figure) in the Holy Spirit. This double meaning refers to the believer, who in like manner would find oneself a source of life for those who were around them. John goes on to say this figure refers to the Holy Spirit proceeding from the believer. This figure is also found in 1QS 4:21, but here the Holy Spirit is *kime niddah*.

37. Bultmann, *Das Evangelium*, 110n5.

38. Hoskyns, *Fourth Gospel*, 316; Westcott, *Gospel*, 126; Bernard, *Critical and Exegetical Commentary*, 21.

39. Bauer, *Das Johannesevangelium*, 67.

DOUBLE MEANING BASED ON THE ARAMAIC WORD USED
BEHIND OUR GREEK TEXT

A third variation of double meaning comes when we approach the concept of the "Lamb of God" in the Gospel of John (cf. 1:36). No evidence of the double meaning can be found in the text, because there is no Greek word that conveys both meanings of the double meaning Aramaic word. It is not a problem of mistranslation so much as a problem of translation.

Some commentators search for the meaning of ὁ ἀμνὸς τοῦ θεοῦ in a reference to the paschal lamb. In the Gospel of John, Jesus is crucified at the hour the lambs were slaughtered for the Passover, and the early church made much of the comparison between Christ and the Passover lamb.[40] But such a suggestion is not complete by itself, for there is no reference to the forgiveness in connection with the paschal lamb. Some, notably Schlatter, have attempted to bring a union between the paschal lamb and the Jewish *tamid*, the regular Jewish sacrificial offering.[41]

C. H. Dodd introduced another line of thought. He interpreted the "Lamb of God" as the apocalyptic lamb of the book of Revelation, and sees the lamb as not only being sacrificed for the redemption of man, but also as becoming the shepherd of the people of God.[42] While these concepts are united in the Apocalypse of John, we question the propriety of extending this union into the Gospel, because the Gospel uses another related figure to express the role of the Christ as apocalyptic leader of his people (10:1–18).[43]

Many commentators have turned to the suffering servant of Isaiah as a solution for the problem.[44] The most attractive aspect of this image is the fact that the servant of Isaiah 53 "bore the sins of many" (v. 12). While the language is not quite the same, the concepts are quite closely connected. The only other uses of ἀμνὸς τοῦ θεοῦ in the New Testament refer to this passage. Acts 8:32 quotes Isaiah 53:7, as Philip uses the passage as a point of departure for his discussion with the Ethiopian eunuch, and 1 Peter 1:9 compares the blood of Christ to that of a lamb without spot or blemish.

40. Barrett, "Lamb of God," 217.

41. Schlatter, *Der Evangelist Johannes*, 46–47.

42. Dodd, *Interpretation*, 230–38.

43. Schnackenburg, *Das Johannesevangelium*, 326.

44. Barrett, *Gospel*, 146–47; Mollat and Braun, *L'Évangile*, 72; and Strathmann, *Das Evangelium*, 47, are but a few.

Bauer cites references from 2 Clement 16:7 and Barnabas 5:2, which show that the early church understood the Lamb of God in relation to the servant of Isaiah.[45]

Ball seems to have been the first to make the observation that ἀμνὸς τοῦ θεοῦ might come from talya' de'laha', the Aramaic term which would mean both "servant" and "lamb" of God. He considered the translation a mistranslation (wrongly, we believe). He was followed by Burney,[46] who used this approach in his argument that the Gospel was originally of Aramaic origin. Should the correlation between ἀμνὸς and talya' be accepted, it need affirm no more than that the original speaker, John the Baptist, spoke in Aramaic. Jeremias seems to have been the first to have emphasized this particular double meaning.[47] He built his case around the Septuagint's use of παῖς, rather than δοῦλος, to represent the suffering servant. Παῖς may also mean "son." The process from one double meaning term (talya) to another double meaning term (παῖς) is natural.[48]

This double meaning thus implies that John the Baptist spoke the word, talya. By his use of the term, the people listening to him understood that Jesus filled the role of the suffering servant of Isaiah as a lamb slain for the sins of the people. The use of the genitive fits perfectly the expression whereby τοῦ θεοῦ can apply to the servant of God or the Lamb of God. Raymond E. Brown seems to have understood the problem rightly when he says that it revolves around two questions: "First, could John the Baptist have had such an understanding of the Lamb of God; second, could the Evangelist?"[49]

The basic question of whether the Baptist proclaimed the expiatory sacrifice of Jesus as the Christ is one that we cannot answer, as there is no possible way for us to determine if the expiatory death of the suffering servant was a doctrine of pre-Christian Judaism. We have no record of it, but it is not impossible to imagine the connection being diminished as a factor of polemical debates between early Judaism and early Christianity. We do know, however, that the early church very soon held Jesus to be the servant of God. In addition to the places which we have already cited and the use of παῖς (Acts 3:13, 26; 4:27, 30), this word was applied to the suffering

45. Bauer, "ἀμνὸς," 45–46.

46. Burney, Aramaic Origin, 107–08.

47. Jeremias, "ἀμνὸς τοῦ θεοῦ/—παῖς θεοῦ," 115–28.

48. Jeremias, "ἀμνὸς τοῦ θεοῦ/—παῖς θεοῦ," 122.

49. Brown, Gospel According to John (i–xii), 60.

servant in Matthew 12:18, a quotation of a passage (Isa 42:1) dealing with the servant.

C. H. Dodd rejects the use of the double meaning term because we have no record of *talya'* being translated with ἀμνός.[50] The word is only translated by ἄρην and ἀρνίον. Two things weaken this argument. First are the observations of Stendahl, showing the Matthean use of Old Testament quotations.[51] In dealing with Matthew 12:18 (a quotation of a servant passage, Isa 42:1), Stendahl shows that there is maximum freedom in the choice of terms. Matthew chooses παῖς over δοῦλος, when παῖς appears only in one extant Greek translation of the Old Testament passage, that of Theodotian. Ἀγαπητός replaces ἐκλεκτός when it appears in no extant Greek manuscript of the Old Testament. A synonym such as *talya'* could come into use and be accepted if it conveyed the meaning needed. We may also note a fluidity in titles used in the Gospel of John. The disciple whom Jesus loved is called μαθητὴν ὃν ἐφίλει (20:2) and μαθητὴν ὃν ἠγάπα ὁ Ἰησοῦς (13:23; 19:26; 21:7). Synonyms may thus easily be exchanged.

In addition to this fluidity of terminology, John the Baptist could have used a double meaning very easily. We find such a usage in the Qumran Habakkuk Commentary (1QpHab 1:9), where the east wind is interpreted as applying to the faces of the people. The environment and milieu of John the Baptist seem to be very much like that of Qumran.

The question of whether the evangelist could have had such an understanding is much less complicated. The interpretation of the early church leaves very little question. The problem the evangelist faced is the same that modern translators face when they come to a double meaning. They must struggle with the problem of bringing a translation that conveys the meaning given by the original author and maintains the spirit of what he said. With this in mind, John probably chose the term "lamb" rather than a term for "servant" because he knew that the former would convey the meaning of both terms to the church, while the latter would not.

DOUBLE MEANING IN A SHORT PERICOPE OR PARABOLIC SAYING

The author of the Gospel of John has developed a use of a short parabolic saying that involves the double meaning. This use relies on a primary

50. Dodd, *Interpretation*, 235–36.
51. Stendahl, *School of St. Matthew*, 109.

meaning of the words for the literal part of the saying. The application or figurative element comes from a secondary meaning of the words. Both aspects of the parabolic saying are bound up with actual meaning of the same words.

A good illustration of this is found in the word ἀκολουθέω. First and third meanings from Bauer are: (1) "come after," with a transition to the figurative meaning of (3) "follow someone as a disciple," with "follow me" equaling "be my disciple," as in Matthew 9:9.[52] An illustration of the double meaning appears in the use of ἀκολουθέω in 8:12: "I am the light of the world. Whoever follows me will never walk in darkness, but will have the light of life." In this passage, John uses the primary meaning of the words as an illustration of the secondary meaning, which he intends as more important. The primary meaning pictures a person walking behind or with Christ, walking with assurance, for one does not walk where one cannot see. The secondary meaning shows this person who has given oneself to Christ as his disciple (or follower) walking in the patterns of behavior set by the Christ with the light of this pattern. He or she walks with the assurance of the first. The one aspect is not complete without the other; both are conveyed by the same words.

We may also note ἀκολουθέω used with the same double meaning in John 1:37–42. In this pericope, we first note the emphasis upon the actual event, for "Jesus turns and sees the men following him." Their action of coming after him is firmly intended. Yet the author is not content to leave us there. In verse 40 we find Andrew, one of those following (ἀκολουθησάντων) him, seeking out his brother and proclaiming his faith: "We have found the Messiah." The emphasis is made even clearer in the following pericope. Here Jesus calls Philip with ἀκολούθει μοι ("follow me"), and Philip seeks out his friend, Nathanael. Thus, it becomes clear that the first action of following was not intended to imply that the disciples merely followed Jesus, but that they also came to a decision that made them disciples (followers). Both elements are actively present. Bultmann is correct when he notes the use of both the physical act of following Jesus and the commitments involved in becoming a disciple.[53]

We should not infer by this that each use should be considered a case of double meaning. John 6:2 simply denotes that people came after Jesus

52. Bauer, "ἀκολουθέω," 30.

53. Bultmann, *Das Evangelium*, 68n5; cf. Westcott, *Gospel*, 24; Schnackenburg, *Das Johannesevangelium*, 308, Hoskyns, *Fourth Gospel*, 179.

because of the curiosity that developed from the signs of healing. Thus, each case must be evaluated individually.

Another short parabolic saying is found in John 3:8: "The wind [πνεῦμα] blows wherever it pleases. You hear its sound, but you cannot tell where it comes from or where it is going. So it is with everyone born of the Spirit [πνεῦμα]." This double meaning has a direct parallel in Ecclesiastes 11:5, where πνεύματος carries the same ambiguity between the wind and spirit as we find in the Gospel of John.

Bernard shows the possibility of translating not only the noun πνεῦμα as "wind," or "spirit," but also that the verb πνέω adequately describes the action of either the wind or the spirit. Even though he rejects the double meaning he says: "There is no etymological objection to translating 'The wind blows where it will and thou hearest its sound,' but we may equally well translate, 'The Spirit breathes where He will and thou hearest His voice.'"[54]

The double meaning cannot apply to those γεγεννημένος ἐκ τοῦ πνεύματος,[55] as there is no intention by the author to imply that these are born of the wind. This is the application of the saying, and the author would not want any to miss the point. While the primary meaning must refer to the wind blowing where it will, the secondary meaning, bound up with the very same words, refers to the free, uninhibited movement of the Spirit of God in the rebirth of those entering his kingdom.

Thus, again we find a word picture and its meaning so closely united that they cannot be separated, even as they are described with the same words. The unseen action of the wind expresses the unknowable actions of the Spirit. The figure is not described with symbolic language, nor is the application. Both come from the actual meanings of the words. With Barrett,

> The allegory in this verse is therefore so close that it depends not upon a symbolical meaning attached to a word or group of words but upon different meanings properly belonging to one word. We may translate either: The wind blows where it wills and you hear the sound of it, but you do not know whence it comes and whither it goes; or, The Spirit breathes where he wills and you hear his voice, but you do not know, etc. Each of these translations taken

---

54. Bernard, *Critical and Exegetical Commentary*, 107.
55. Zahn, *Das Evangelium des Johannes*, 188.

by itself is wrong . . . the double meaning simply cannot be repro-
duced in English.[56]

This close union of terminology brings about the dilemma of the transla-
tor once more. The situation presents no problem in the Hebrew, Aramaic,
Syriac, or Greek, where the words for "wind" and "spirit" are the same. But
when we come to the Latin, we leave these languages where the terminology
permits the double meaning. Thus, the Latin translators have been forced
to make a choice. They chose "the Spirit blows where it wills" (*Spiritus ubi
vult spirat*), but immediately the double meaning is lost. The English Bible
translators have been forced to make a similar choice that usually results in
"the wind blows where it wills," also losing the force of the double meaning.
One of the deficiencies of translation comes when we attempt to bring out
the full meaning of terminology into languages where such terminology
does not carry exactly the same connotations that the original carried.

This same phenomenon is at work in the pericope on judgment in
3:19–21. In this passage, the parallel is drawn between the good person and
the evil man. The good man is not concerned about others knowing about
his actions because they are in line with his reputation. The evil man does
not want others to know what he is doing because he knows it is wrong.
These actions are usually done at night or in seclusion. Yet behind this figure of light is Jesus Christ. He is the light who has come into the world (1:8,
14; 8:12; 9:5). The world will be judged by its relation to him (3:16, 18), as
he is the standard of right and good. As in the previous passage the author
has chosen the verb ἐλεγχθῇ, which has a secondary meaning that fits the
meaning of the parabolic laying.[57]

Yet this passage is not a true case of double meaning, for while Christ
is the light of the world, and readers must not fail to miss this point, the
inference is not drawn from a primary and secondary meaning of the word,
but from the primary meaning and the author's metaphor. The latter is not
truly a secondary meaning, although the use of metaphor is one of the chief
causes of new meaning for words. Certainly, the early Christian would not
have missed this metaphor. It fulfills the function of double meaning we
have seen in 3:8, 7:39, and 8:12 by laying a parabolic background for the
meaning that the author wishes to convey. We should thus be cautious to
note the distinction between the use of the word and the author's ability to
expect his readers to find the double meaning.

56. Barrett, *Gospel*, 175.
57. Gingrich, "Ambiguity," 77.

DOUBLE MEANING OF VERBS BASED ON MODE

Gingrich has noted another form of double meaning. The ambiguity found in various verb forms, particularly the second person plural, may be indicative or imperative.[58] He infers that both of these modes of a verb are meant to apply in such cases.

We might note the case of John 8:38: "I am telling you what I have seen in the Father' presence and you do [ποιεῖτε] what you have heard from your Father." By its grammatical form, ποιεῖτε may either be imperative or indicative second person plural. Is the verse a declarative statement, or a command? Is Jesus using the imperative, telling the Jews to do the work of their Father (if they really are the children of God), or is he telling them that they are doing the work of their father, and that this work identifies their father? We think both. But translators must choose one or the other. The NIV chooses to follow the indicative. Verse 39 expresses this choice. Jesus said, "If you were Abraham's children, then you would do the things Abraham did." But Jesus then proceeds in his explanation to show that they are seeking to kill him, and this is the work of their father, whom they imitate. Thus, verse 41 claims: "You are doing the things your own father does." The Jews are not seeking to do the work of their Father whom they claim but show themselves to be the children of another father, the devil (v. 44).

The same phenomenon makes itself evident when we turn to 5:39: "You diligently study the Scriptures because you think that by them you possess eternal life. These are the Scriptures that testify about me." Again, the form of the second person plural is the same in the indicative and the imperative. Which does the author mean? Bultmann rejected the imperative, because he felt that θέλετε in verse 40 required the indicative.[59] However, the passage does imply that Jesus wished the Jews to continue their search of the Scriptures to learn about him. Verses 45 and 46 show that Jesus is rather calling them again to the Scriptures to see Moses as the one who testifies concerning him. He cannot be indicating that the Jewish opinion that they shall find life in the Scriptures is wrong (as Bernard thinks),[60] for these verses show Moses as the chief witness to Jesus as the Christ. Thus, life was available to those who through the Scriptures came to know the Christ, of whom Moses wrote.

58. Gingrich, "Ambiguity," 77.

59. Bultmann, *Das Evangelium*, 201n4.

60. Bernard, *Critical and Exegetical Commentary*, 253.

The evangelist pictures the words of Jesus as not only noting the Jews' open study of the Scripture (the indicative use), but also commends (the imperative use) them to continue in this search, for they shall find that Moses is the chief witness to the life and the role Jesus is leading. If the Jews would come to a true understanding of the Scripture (as believers had), they would see the Scripture as witness to Jesus as the Christ, and they would find life in Moses' words.

This same double meaning may come into effect in 14:1: "Do not let your hearts be troubled. Trust in God; trust also in me." Gingrich suggests these verbs both be translated in the same mode: "You believe in God (naturally, since you are Jews), therefore believe also in me," or, "Believe (truly) in God (as I reveal him), and you will also believe in me."[61] C. K. Barrett brings three possible combinations: indicative-indicative, imperative-imperative, and indicative-imperative, which he considers possible from the context. Then he notes: "None of these variations is repugnant to the sense of the passage as a whole but the imperative $\tau\alpha\rho\alpha\sigma\sigma\acute{\epsilon}\sigma\theta\omega$ suggests that the later verbs may be imperatives also."[62] We have indications from the text for the acceptance of the double meaning, as we have noted in the other situations.

Another possible double meaning of this type is 15:18, where $\gamma\iota\nu\acute{\omega}\sigma\kappa\epsilon\tau\epsilon$ is used. Here there does not seem to be much difference between the meaning of the indicative and the imperative. The indicative would suggest a knowledge the disciples had of the hatred of the world. The imperative would merely commend them to have or keep such knowledge. But both probably apply.

WORDS THAT RELY ON FIGURATIVE MEANING FOR THE AUTHOR'S FULL EXPRESSION

A final variation to the double meaning may be noted when we consider the uses of $\nu\acute{\upsilon}\xi$ in the Gospel of John. The basic difference between this word and the others we have considered is that the double meaning does not rely upon a secondary meaning, but upon a symbolic interpretation. The emphasis of this symbolic interpretation may vary throughout the Gospel. We may come to places where its existence seems to be very elusive, causing us to question whether the evangelist intended a symbolic interpretation. Inasmuch as this section relies on symbolic interpretation rather than

61. Gingrich, "Ambiguity," 77.
62. Barrett, *Gospel*, 380.

true double meaning, we shall be illustrative in our approach rather than exhaustive.

When we consider uses of νύξ in the Gospel, two passages immediately fall into a pattern. We noted the ability of the evangelist to lay a figure of speech in a small parable that had double meaning. This emphasis is found in 9:4–5, but the meaning is bound up not in the meanings of the word, but in an obvious figurative meaning. Thus the author says: "As long as it is day, we must do the work of him who sent me. Night [νύξ] is coming when no one can work. While I am in the world, I am the Light of the World." The symbolic use of day and night refers to the life and the coming death of Jesus. As one works only when it is day and rests during the night, so Jesus can only work while he lives. His coming death will end his mission on earth.[63]

We may note much the same thing in 11:9–11: "Jesus answered, 'Are there not twelve hours of daylight? A man who walks by day will not stumble, for he sees by this world's light. It is when he walks by night [νύξ] that he stumbles, for he has no light.'" The symbolic interpretation here is that of light and darkness, rather than looking to the coming death of Jesus. Schlatter points out a quotation from Rabba Exodus to show that this figure was used in Jewish circles with the law as the light.[64] In this passage, the emphasis is rather on the moral teaching of Jesus as the light that he brought into the world. It is this morality that is missing within a person's life and results in them walking in darkness. Without it, as without the law, one stumbles and falls.

The other uses of night are not a part of such parabolic forms. They are simply a part of the narrative. The most obvious double meaning is that of 13:30, where the symbolic emphasis is given by the author when he says "ἦν δὲ νύξ." The tradition of Scripture is that the betrayal of Jesus took place at night. First Corinthians 11:23 lays emphasis on this meaning, but the implications of John 13:30 seem to go much deeper than merely leaving the gathering while it was dark. "This (use of night) may be only a note of time such as John is apt to give . . . but it is remarkably impressive here, and the dramatic horror of the moment is brought before the reader. Judas went out into the darkness. The symbolic meaning can hardly be absent from the mind of the evangelist."[65] Both aspects seem to have their full force. Not

63. Barrett, *Gospel*, 295; Hoskyns, *Fourth Gospel*, 393.

64. Schlatter, *Der Evangelist Johannes*, 249.

65. Bernard, *Critical and Exegetical Commentary*, 476.

only did Judas go out into darkness of night, but also into the control of the powers of darkness, condemning himself to eternal darkness.

We find the word "νύξ" used twice (and possibly three times if the variant of 7:50 found in the Western Text is correct) in connection with the coming of Nicodemus. These passages come to us with much less certainty regarding their symbolic meaning than do those we have previously considered. Raymond E. Brown asserts that the recall of the detail is made because of its symbolic importance.[66] Two things weaken this argument. First is the fact that night is not always used with the same symbolic meaning, as we have seen in 9:4, where it referred to the coming death of Jesus. In 11:10 and 13:30, it refers to the Johannine structure between light and darkness. The only other use, 21:3, has been symbolized to indicate the failure to catch fish during the night, but it also may merely indicate that the night is the best time to fish, and the disciples, as skillful fishermen, were making the best use of their time.[67] John 21:3, if seen symbolically, would contradict the symbolism of 9:4, where it suggests that night brings a cessation from labor. The "symbolic" interpretation would suggest that Jesus' death or departure was considered darkness. His return brings the light of morning again. But even if this is accepted, we must note the two strains of symbolism in the use of night.

Second, the author uses identifying phrases in other places merely for purposes of identification. John 11:2 identifies Mary as "This Mary, whose brother Lazarus now lay sick, was the same one who poured perfume on the Lord and wiped his feet with her hair." This is certainly a means of identifying Mary, rather than a means of expressing symbolism in her action. The author uses this same type of identification with Caiaphas (18:14) and the beloved disciple (21:20). The historical notes to Nicodemus seem to be the same, and they may simply refer to his coming after dark. The textual variant (7:50) may possibly allow νύξ to come in as the original text, but we believe the Nestle text is correct in not preferring it to the other stronger readings. Thus, in 7:50 the author identifies Nicodemus without the key symbolic word; 19:39 carries no more weight than the identification of Nicodemus, paralleling 11:2, 18:14, and 21:20.

When we face the symbolic uses of the Gospel, we cannot deny their existence, but we must come to them with extreme caution lest we read more into the text than the author intended. There are many good reasons

66. Brown, *Gospel According to John (xiii–xxi)*, 130.
67. Bruns, "Use of Time," 290.

why Nicodemus should have come to see Jesus by night. In addition to the sinister aspects of night, Hoskyns suggests the Jewish desire to discuss the law by night and the solitude.[68] Westcott sees the timidity with regard to the Jewish authorities.[69] While C. K. Barrett may be right in connecting the coming by night with the contrast between light and darkness at the conclusion of the discourse (vv. 19–21), we see no necessity for this interpretation.[70]

Each individual symbolic use must be considered on its own merit. We cannot fall into the trap of making the author use certain words with and only with a symbolic meaning. This sharply limits his mode of self-expression. We have seen double meaning with ἄνωθεν in 3:3, but not with the other uses of this term in the Gospel. We have found double meaning with πνεῦμα in 3:8, but no one would suggest that, each time πνεῦμα is used in the Gospel, the wind is involved.

Another caution we should consider as we define the extent of the double meaning in the Gospel of John are the cases where the symbolic or secondary meaning comes in such a way that the primary meaning drops out of use all together. In 11:11–14, κεκοίμηται may mean both "to sleep" and "to die" when referring to the death of Lazarus. Oscar Cullmann sees a possible double meaning here, with the higher meaning death took on for the Christian regarding the resurrection of Lazarus.[71] Yet if this be the case, the first meaning is then missing. It is true that, with Christ, we have a new teaching regarding death, but we cannot have both involved here.

In conclusion, we have explored the main uses of double meaning in John. While each use is different and must be considered on its own individual basis, the general patterns that the double meaning follows are clear. The use of two clearly definable meanings of a word becomes important in each case. The double meaning is not an allegorical approach. It is not related to hidden meanings, but that which the evangelist reveals through his choice of words. It shows how the words of the text are carefully, not carelessly, chosen and how they bring new depth of meaning to the text. The double meaning is a refinement of the technique the author used by which he developed the historical and interpretative elements of his theology. Should we have desired to separate them there, we could not. Neither

---

68. Hoskyns, *Fourth Gospel*, 211.

69. Westcott, *Gospel*, 48.

70. Barrett, *Gospel*, 170.

71. Cullmann, *Urchristentum und Gottesdienst*, 54n15d.

is such a separation possible here, as they are bound so closely that they are a part of the same word. The same word brings both meanings to mind, and such is the function of this literary device.

CHAPTER 4

IRONY IN THE FOURTH GOSPEL

When Bishop Connop Thirlwall wrote "On the Irony of Sophocles," he not only set the terminology often used in literary criticism, but he also pointed us to ancient Greece for the source of the discussion of irony.[1] So although the terminology and the ideas discussed in this portion of the work are modern, we can trace the roots into the pre-Christian era.

THE USE OF IRONY IN CLASSICAL ANTIQUITY

With Plato and the Greek tragedists, irony was normally presented in the form of a contest (ἀγών) between two types of characters. The imposter or boaster (ἀλάζων) would come, making himself more than he really was. Such a man was encountered by the εἴρων, who would make less of his case than it really deserved. This εἴρων always proved able to cope with the situation and to be more than the fool he pretended to be.[2] As Cicero expressed it: the former simulates, the latter dissimulates.[3]

The most illustrious εἴρων of this era is undoubtedly Socrates. In fact, his use of irony and the low esteem that his countrymen placed upon the method led to his downfall. It was only when Plato presented his teacher in a more positive light that the term lost some of its negative connotations.[4]

The *New Century Dictionary* defines irony as:

> A method of expression or a figure of speech in which the literal meaning of the words is the opposite of the thought in the

---

1. Thirlwall, "Irony of Sophocles."
2. Thomson, *Irony*, 10.
3. Cicero, *De Officiis*, 1.30.
4. Cornford, *Origin of Attic Comedy*, 161.

speaker's mind and intended to be conveyed, and which is employed in ridicule or contempt or merely playfully; . . . an outcome of events contrary to what was or what might have been expected.[5]

To this, Cicero simply said *"dicere aliud ac sentias."*[6] Irony involves the disparity between the meaning conveyed and the literal meanings of the words as stated.

When authors use irony, they understate their case. They usually do this through the disparity between the understanding of the character in the play and the meaning the audience perceives. Thus, the character speaks that which is truth within his or her understanding, but the audience understands it in relation to the total context of the drama. The conflict pictures a discrepancy between "the appearance" that one sees on the stage and the "reality" that is really known. "The proper signification of the words constitutes the appearance; the designed meaning is the reality!"[7]

The use of irony, of course, requires an author to hold a theological or philosophical view of the universe against which the conflict can be dramatized. The Greek tragedian did not hesitate to make his religious or philosophical feelings known. "Ironic tragedy, then, comprehends the tragic fate in terms of an assumption about the meaning of the world on the basis, as I have suggested before, of a vision of truth."[8]

The author assumes a "godlike" position. He or she considered the events narrated with a view of what is true and right and the reasons for the consequences of the wrong actions of those involved. The irony thus comes when we would see the "appearance" that the characters understand against the "reality" to which the author is leading us. The plot of the drama is completely under his wide sweeping vision and his complete control. He "creates" the whole scope that is before us.

In this manner, the author may write the irony into the parts of the characters, or it may become a part of the author's complete portrayal. A character like Socrates works to dissimulate his adversaries by attacking them in an ironical manner. This form of irony places him against his unwitting and unwilling opponents with questions that make these "knowing" adversaries admit the truth.

---

5. Emery and Brewster, *New Century Dictionary*, 859.

6. Cicero, as quoted in Sedgewick, *Of Irony*, 8.

7. Sedgewick, *Of Irony*, 9.

8. Good, *Irony in the Old Testament*, 25–26.

In the alternative method, the author assumes a quasi-divine attitude which exhibits a freedom from the contradictions of life, and like an artist he or she exhibits a creative power giving shape to the spectacle the audience observes.[9] In *Oedipus Rex*, the words of Oedipus carry the irony of his own blindness to the truth that the killer whom he seeks is none other than himself.[10]

If such irony is to be understood by the audience, it must come in relation to the entire context. The meanings of the various statements cannot be taken from the text alone, but rather must be drawn from the entire context from which the author writes. The immediate context only supplies one side of the double-edged expression. It only brings us to the significance the words held for those in that context and who were limited by it. It cannot bring us to the irony the author intended to convey. This can only come from an understanding of the significance the author wished to give to the entire drama.[11]

There would seem to be a relation between the comic and the tragic in irony. We cannot overlook a certain comic element, as the haughty Jews speak against their God. But while irony may involve the comic, it usually participates in a sense of pain enough that it ceases to be humorous.[12] It involves this sense of pain in such a way that the discrepancy between the appearance and the reality are used to entertain the audience.

While with Thompson we allow that this comic element does exist in irony, we should caution ourselves not to make the mistake Jónsson has made with his close alignment of humor and irony: "if the irony is to be correctly estimated, it must be quite clear that it is understood as a joke."[13] We believe that Mr. Jónsson would come to a more comprehensive understanding of irony if he should follow the Aristotelian position he set forth with his discussion of paradox. Aristotle's definition of irony is in relation to truth, and not humor. The comic element is only incidental.

This strong comic element may come from the fact that Jónsson and Clavier (whom he seems to follow) rely heavily on Plato's presentation of Socrates for their position with little consideration of the Greek Tragedists and Aristotle. This idealistic position seems to be based on French literary

9. Thirlwall, as quoted in Thompson, *Dry Mock*, 143–48.

10. Sedgewick, *Of Irony*, 20.

11. Brooks, "Irony as a Principle," 731.

12. Thompson, *Dry Mock*, 47.

13. Jónsson, *Humour and Irony*, 22. Cf. Clavier, "L'Ironie," 261.

criticism, principally that of Vladimir Jankelevitch and Haury.[14] The one-sidedness of this approach allows these authors to overlook much of the irony we find in the Gospel of John. Clavier thus makes irony *"une certaine maniere de questioner."* In doing this, he justly points to the pattern for irony we find in Socrates.

However, in so doing, he wrongly places the emphasis upon Socrates and directs us completely away from the method of Sophocles and the Greek stage, where the term gained its meaning. These dramatists were equally adept as ironists, although their characters were not. The Greek tragedists developed irony not as questioners, but as authors who controlled the true meaning of events. When one observes the characters of Sophocles, Aeschylus, and Euripides, they are not using irony as a weapon, as Socrates did. Rather, their irony comes in their words, the true meaning of which the characters themselves do not understand. The conflict is between the meaning the character perceives and the total meaning of the plot; the latter is the meaning the author wished to convey.

Irony is then a statement (usually an understatement) or an action by which the author or character intends to convey another meaning than that which the words superficially carry. This deeper meaning regards the truth of the narrative, and such a meaning in literature will usually come from the entire context rather than the immediate context. Because there may be an unexpected twist in what we would expect, we may sense a comic element, but the pain involved prevents the twist from being truly humorous.

PREREQUISITES FOR EFFECTIVE IRONY

The godlike position of the author is one of the key marks of irony. This position controls the relationship with the characters and the audience. It is through these relationships that the author must work to present his irony and convey its meaning. Bishop Thirlwall expressed this in his article from the early nineteenth century: "The dramatist must view his mimic world as he supposes the Creator to view the real world, and the essential character of his poetry will therefore depend on his religious sentiments."[15] In this same vein of thought, J. A. K. Thomson notes: "There is in Aristophanes a conscious intellectual superiority to his puppets, even when he is the most

---

14. Jankélévitch, *L'Ironie*; Haury, *L'Ironie*.
15. Thirlwall, as quoted in Thompson, *Dry Mock*, 143.

sympathetic."[16] This superiority allows him to perceive the true meaning in the events. He raises himself above the clouds and mists of earthly existence, and comes to a position where he can truly comprehend the meaning behind the errors and wanderings of men.[17]

The relation between the author and the audience is not only essential for the communication of irony, but also is one of the great differences between modern and ancient drama. In the ancient drama, the events involved in the plot were completely known to the audience. People did not go to the play to see how it would come out, but rather to see how the author would handle the events that were well-known to them. Sophocles, Aeschylus, and Euripides wrote dramas dealing with the same historical events. "It was to the ordinary Greek spectator an historical fact that Clytemnestra slew Agamemnon and that Oedipus married Iocasta."[18] Aristophanes shows Dicaeopolis in the Achareans saying:

> The audience knowing who I am all right,
> But the Chorus standing by in rows
> Like fools, for me to lead them by the nose.[19]

The audience's foreknowledge was so necessary that prologues and similar devices were used to insure its presence.[20]

But the relation between the author and his audience goes deeper. There must also be a union between author and audience through which the audience can perceive the position of the author in relation to the action on the stage. The author must in some way reveal his or her godlike position if the irony is to be effective.[21]

The success of the author's use of irony as an instrument of persuasion depends upon his or her ability to gain agreement from the audience as to the desirability of their position.[22] When we find this agreement, the effect of the irony can be pleasant; without it, the device can be irritating. The author usually attempts to reveal his or her general position by the handling

16. Thomson, *Irony*, 33.

17. Sedgewick, *Of Irony*, 16.

18. Thomson, *Irony*, 73.

19. As quoted in Thomson, *Irony*, 24.

20. Thomson, *Irony*, 37.

21. Booth, *Rhetoric of Fiction*, 310.

22. Frye, *Anatomy of Criticism*, 224.

of the entire context of the drama in relation to the immediate contexts of the individual scenes.

The second key relationship is between the author and the characters. Irony is displayed between the character's actual situation and the situation in which the character believes oneself to be. "The spectators know the facts, the people in the play do not. A character's actual situation is one thing, his idea or interpretation of it is another; the promise things have for him is at variance with their outcome—they are not what they seem."[23] Thus Thirlwall noted a special bit of irony from *Oedipus Rex*: "In the scene with Tiresias, Oedipus taunts the latter with his blindness. The 'practical irony' of the outcome is that Oedipus blinds himself."[24] This blindness must be a part of any written work where the characters are pictured as actual living creatures. It is a part of all life. We do not know the meaning of the situation wherein we stand. However, in dramatic writing where the author assumes a special godlike position, the author can make known the true meaning of any situation. There is thus a strong possibility that the discrepancy will exist between the understanding of the character and the truth the author pictures. This discrepancy allows for the skillful author to incorporate irony into the work.

The third relationship involves the author and his or her work. In the chapter on the literary point of view, we have shown that the point of view controls the purpose for which the author writes.

> First of all, there are three different points of view toward an irony: that of the person using it for attack, that of its victim, and that of the onlooker. If our view is that of the attacker we shall probably feel no sympathy but rather rejoice at the discomfiture we cause. Contrariwise, if we are the victim we shall hardly be amused at all. The action becomes ironical in its full sense only when we have the onlooker's view.[25]

This onlooker's view is comparable to the third-person point of view defined in first chapter of this work.

Herein lies the difference between the irony of Socrates and that of Sophocles. Socrates fulfills the role of the attacker, who uses his irony to attack that which he feels to be pretentious and false in his opponents. His victims feel his irony as something very unpleasant, for it destroys their

---

23. Sedgewick, *Of Irony*, 25–26.

24. Thompson, *Dry Mock*, 145.

25. Thompson, *Dry Mock*, 19–20.

position. This was not the case with the Sophoclean approach. He writes from the position of the audience. His purpose was to draw the audience to the real truth of the situation, and through this truth to lead them to understand their own situation in life more correctly. "But the basis of irony in a vision of truth means that irony aims at amendment of the incongruous rather than its annihilation."[26]

IRONY IN THE GOSPEL OF JOHN

Our purpose in this work is to go beyond Socrates to Sophocles as we seek to understand the irony of the Gospel of John. In the Gospel you must not only consider the context we find Jesus teaches and deals with people but also that which John finds to be the reality of the larger context.

The necessary elements are present for the author to use irony effectively. The first of these is the position of the author. The evangelist has taken the godlike position over his work and his characters so that he can present the reality of the events, compared to the apparent meaning evident to those who participated in the events. This double-edged understanding comes from the author's view of his own inspiration.

The Holy Spirit is working through him in a special way to bring the true meaning of the events that have taken place. The term "godlike," which Thirlwall used to describe the position of the author, becomes more expressive of the position of our author. John can act, in a very real sense, with creativity, because the Spirit of God is with him, guiding him to the true understanding of what happened.

Irony was natural for the evangelist because of his use of dual meanings and the concept of the divine revelation of God. The former placed him in a vein where he was prone to see both the historical (what happened) and the interpretive (what it meant). The irony comes when we see the disparity between the historical and the interpretative. John's emphasis upon the historical leads us to see the ignorance of those on the stage who dealt with Jesus and the deeper meaning available to the reader and author. This deeper meaning was possible because the Spirit was to guide the apostle.

The relation to the audience is equally clear. "More than any other gospel, John [20:31] states in salvific terms the purpose for which it was written."[27] "These things were written that you may believe that Jesus is the

26. Good, *Irony in the Old Testament*, 27.
27. Brown, "Kerygma of the Gospel," 387.

Christ, the Son of God, and that by believing you may have life in his name" (John 20:31). The discussion of the textual variant allowing for the use of the aorist verb "πιστεύσητε" does shed some light on this relation. If the audience is made up of believing Christians whose faith should be strengthened (the use of the present tense), there would be implied a union between the author and his audience. If the audience is primarily non-Christian and is being called to the faith (the use of the aorist), there is no present union between the author and his audience, but such a union is sought. While the use of the present tense is stronger and probably correct, we cannot see in it more than the primary purpose of the Gospel. The irony would be effective only for those who accept the position of the author. If they should not accept his position, there need not be a discrepancy between the appearance and the reality. The appearance could be the reality. The realization of the presence of irony depends upon the union of thought between the author and his audience.

The relation between the author and his or her chief character is just as clear. In addition to the stated purpose (20:31), the author uses a prologue (John 1:1–18), which the ancient authors often used to remove any doubt the audience might have as to the events the author was to relate. He presented Jesus as nothing short of God, θεὸς ἦν ὁ λόγος. He claimed to have been an eyewitness to the events of the life of Jesus here on earth during which he "beheld his divinity" (δόξαν ὡς μονογενοῦς παρὰ πατρός; v. 14). He saw the one greater than Moses who had brought grace and truth (v. 17). Jesus had seen the Father and had made the Father known to them (v. 18). John is closely united with the character whom he presents. Jesus is the God whom he worships.

The relation of the author to the remaining characters varies with the relation they have to the main character. The author's position is that of the main character. Through the other characters, much of the irony of the Gospel is revealed. Very little of it comes through the actual words of Jesus.

> The opponents of Jesus are given to making statements about him that are derogatory, sarcastic, incredulous, or at least inadequate in the sense they were intended. However, by way of irony these statements are often true and more meaningful in a sense they do not realize. The evangelist simply presents these statements and leaves them unanswered (or answered with an eloquent silence)

for he is certain that his believing readers will see the deeper truth (cf. 4:12; 7:35, 42; 8:22; 11:50).[28]

THE METHOD OF THE AUTHOR

We shall note three approaches to the use of irony found in the Fourth Gospel. These three approaches vary with the amount of certainty there is that the author is depending on the superior knowledge of the audience. The first, the so-called "wink," is a device wherein the author takes pains to step aside and explain the irony he or she puts into the text. This is done from the author's godlike position. The second approach is one whereby the author relies upon the superior knowledge he supplies us at other places. The complete context of the Gospel reveals the intent of what is said. The final approach is when the superior knowledge of the audience is supposed to come from sources outside the Gospel of John. Of course, the surety of the use of irony varies directly with the surety of the audience's superior knowledge.

The so-called "wink" comes when the author relates to the readers that there is a second and fuller meaning to what has been said. Probably the most striking use of this form of irony comes in 11:50–52. This passage is built around the statement of Caiaphas: "You do not realize that it is better for you that one man die for the people than that the whole nation perish" (v. 50). Caiaphas meant this statement to have political connotations alone. For him, the political situation was serious. Another in the line of Messianic revolutionaries had arisen. This Messianic figure had come with signs meant to authenticate his claim. But these signs had led the leadership of the Jewish nation to believe he was a false prophet.[29] Now there was a possibility that those in Galilee who accepted his claim would attempt to make king (6:15). The movement was gaining strength, and Caiaphas feared that this move to make him king could spread to Judea. With larger groups following Jesus every day, it was alarming to think of the consequences that might arise if the Romans should consider this a revolution or if it should develop into one. Caiaphas was giving a common sense political solution to the tense situation that lay before him.

28. Brown, *Gospel According to John (i–xii)*, cxxxvi.

29. See Wead, "We Have a Law," 185–89.

The evangelist emphasizes a deeper meaning to these words, a meaning Caiaphas himself did not realize. His own prophecy was given without his knowledge. Jesus was to die on behalf of Israel, but not politically. He was to be their spiritual Savior.[30] Thus the author gives us the "wink," showing us the real meaning as contrasted with the meaning Caiaphas intended: "He did not say this on his own, but as high priest that year he prophesied that Jesus would die for the Jewish nation, and not only for that nation but for the scattered children of God, to bring them together and make them one" (vv. 51–52). The deep irony of the situation lies in the fact that, through the death of Jesus, exactly that result the high priest was attempting to prevent came to pass. The death of Jesus, the rejection of the true Messiah, is that which caused the doom of the nation. "Johannine irony scarcely reaches a higher point. Jesus was put to death; and (politically) the people perished. Yet he died ὑπὲρ τοῦ ἔθνους and those of the nation who believed in him did not perish (ἵνα πᾶς ὁ πιστεύων εἰς αὐτὸν μὴ ἀπόληται) but received eternal life (3:16)."[31]

The second approach to irony, which depends upon the supplied superior knowledge of the audience, can be illustrated with 7:48. This mode differs, in that the author does not make the disparity of the irony known expressly. Rather, he depends upon the knowledge he has given the audience in other places to show them the contrast between appearance and reality. Thus, when the servants return from the arrest attempt emptyhanded, the Pharisees retort, "You mean he has deceived you also?" In Greek, their question is as follows: μή τις ἐκ τῶν ἀρχόντων ἐπίστευσεν εἰς αὐτὸν ἢ ἐκ τῶν Φαρισαίων? The rhetorical question is so stated that only a negative answer is possible.[32] The use of μή emphasizes the strong belief of the leaders that, of their number, none had become disciples of Jesus.

The audience knows that this is not the truth. They have seen the visit of Nicodemus in chapter 3. While there is a question of his coming to faith, the author's record of the speech of Nicodemus (v. 50) is meant to call attention to this previous visit.[33] This discrepancy between the appearance of the situation to those who led the Jews and its reality becomes even more clear in 12:42. Here John notes: "Yet at the same time many even among the

30. Brown, *Gospel According to John (i–xii)*, 442; Lightfoot, *St. John's Gospel*, 227–228.

31. Barrett, *Gospel*, 339.

32. Blass et al., *Greek Grammar*, §440, 226.

33. Bultmann, *Das Evangelium*, 235; cf. also Brown, *Gospel According to John (i–xii)*, 325.

leaders believed in him. But, because of the Pharisees they would not con-
fess their faith for fear they would be put out of the synagogue." The short
period of time that elapsed (Tishrei to Nisan is the period between the
Feast of Tabernacles and the Feast of Passover, which is about six months)
makes it quite possible that the number of believers who were in the same
camp as Nicodemus was large, even at this point.[34]

The third approach the author uses to show the device of irony involves a supposition of the audience's superior knowledge. This presupposes knowledge of the other gospel traditions and other earlier works of
the New Testament.[35] This supposition was active in the tradition of the
descent of the Holy Spirit upon Jesus in the form of the dove. The Synoptics
connect this act with the baptism of Jesus, but John only recorded the event
as having taken place (1:31–34).

In 11:16 Thomas uttered his cry of desperation and devotion: "Let us
go that we may die with him." The irony of the statement is so strong that
C. K. Barrett doubts that the proposal rests upon early tradition.[36] Yet the
situation John portrays is so plausible, we wonder why such doubts should
arise. The fate of disciples was tied very closely to that of their Master (John
18:8, although Acts 5:36–37 seems to indicate the Jews felt it was enough
to slay the leader and disperse the disciples.). The minds of Jesus' disciples
could not help but connect their fate with that which they suspected for
him. "Here Thomas foresaw only too clearly that Jesus was going to his
death, and he realized that to enter Judea as His disciple was to risk the
same fate. But Jesus was his Master, and he would not draw back when he
found that Jesus was resolved to go back to Judea."[37]

The meaning of the text undoubtedly goes much deeper. The disciples
did truly die, but it was not the kind of death they expected. The devotion of
Thomas ironically points us to the devoted "deaths" the apostles really did
die. Their trip to Jerusalem resulted in such complete commitment of life
that the New Testament writers could only describe it as "death." Thomas
did not see anything beyond the danger they faced when they accompanied
Jesus to Jerusalem. Herein lies the irony. The author presents the words of
Thomas as carrying more meaning than they originally carried to Thomas.
As Jesus died, the events of the Passion would lead the apostles to the same

34. Hoskyns, *Fourth Gospel*, 325.
35. Salmon, *Historical Introduction*, 275–85.
36. Barrett, *Gospel*, 327.
37. Bernard, *Critical and Exegetical Commentary*, 381.

commitment Jesus showed, to stand willing to die for their faith. We, with the author, can see the larger context in which the statement is written.[38]

Of these approaches the last two are by far more prevalent. The places where the evangelist tells us how the mistakes are to be corrected are rare (only 2:20 and 11:52).[39] John himself provides the most help by not allowing his ironic passages to stand alone. Rather they fall into groups that follow themes. The number of passages combined into these ironic themes and the similarities of the author's style in presenting them give strength to our understanding of them as irony. Let us now turn to examine how these three approaches to irony are developed in the remainder of the Gospel.

THEMES IN THE GOSPEL OF JOHN WHERE IRONY IS USED

The main uses of irony in the Gospel of John fall into themes that move through various phases of the Gospel. These themes rest upon the supposition that the reader, who has superior knowledge, is aware of the real truth of the situation. Each of these themes revolves around a truth the author wishes to emphasize. Through the irony, he is able to define in a negative sense the concept with which he is dealing and concentrate his thought upon the development of the theme.

The King of the Jews

The ironic use of this theme is found in the accounts of the trial and crucifixion of Jesus. In the Synoptic accounts, this aspect of the final events of the life of Jesus is important, but not so important as we find in the Gospel of John. Here the events of the trial echo again and again with the theme, "Jesus is the King of the Jews!" John is confident the Christian who reads his Gospel will agree, "Yes, Jesus is the King of the Jews," and will understand the events that are found therein in this light. The irony comes when we examine the way things appear to those who were a part of the events and the reality of the events we know. We can see the deeper meaning.

The trial scene is paradoxical. Pilate believes that he is the judge. The Jewish leadership believes that they are the accusers. In the end, Pilate is

38. Bultmann, *Das Evangelium*, 305; cf. Barrett, *Gospel*, 327.
39. Bernard, *Critical and Exegetical Commentary*, xxxiv.

judged, and the Jews stand before their Christ as the ones accused.[40] We may note the same type of paradoxical situation in chapter 9. There, the Pharisees sit in judgment on the claims of Jesus and the blind man to whom sight is given. But in the end, they find the situation changed, and they themselves are the ones who are judged by the truth. However, in the trial of Jesus, this irony reaches its tragic heights. By their blindness, the Jews give up that for which their nation has prepared for centuries. They truly "have no king but Caesar."[41]

John immediately calls our attention to the concept of the kingship of Jesus as Pilate enters the Praetorium to question Jesus. His opening question is: "Are you the King of the Jews?" (18:33). The question becomes the *Stichwort* of the entire chain of events that follow.[42] The answers Jesus gives in the following discussion can lead Pilate to no other position than the fact that Jesus does claim to be a king. Note especially Jesus' response, referring to his kingdom (v. 36), and the response of Pilate in verse 37: "You are a king, then?"

> The particle (οὐκοῦν), which occurs only here in the New Testament, gives a tinge of irony to the words, which are half interrogatory in form and half an explanation: "So then, after all, thou art a king?" This scornful tone is further accentuated by the personal pronoun at the end of the sentence: "Thou, a helpless prisoner."[43]

For the Jews, the term "King of the Jews" undoubtedly held connotations it did not hold for Pilate. For the former, it was the basis for their rejection of Jesus as a false prophet.[44] For Pilate, the title undoubtedly carried more political implications. However, for Jesus, the concept carried still other connotations he now had the opportunity to expand upon.[45] His kingdom is not of this world. He does not seek to be the conquering political ruler the Jews seek. Bultmann notes that the reader knows that Jesus' kingdom is not of this world and that it is above all earthly kingdoms, a heavenly kingdom.[46]

40. Dodd, *Interpretation*, 436.

41. Salmon, *Historical Introduction*, 280; Schlier, "Jesus und Pilatus," 57.

42. Schlier, "Jesus und Pilatus," 60.

43. Westcott, *Gospel*, 260.

44. Meeks, *Prophet King*, 55–57.

45. Blank, "Die Verhandlung vor Pilatus," 69.

46. Bultmann, *Das Evangelium*, 506.

But this bit of superior knowledge is kept in the background. The audience knows that Jesus is king and knows the claims of his kingdom, but Pilate does not. Jesus carefully points out to Pilate the spiritual, non-political nature of his kingdom (18:37). He does not seek the revolution that Pilate considers dangerous to Rome. But more than this, Pilate does not know.

Now the stage is set for the drama to progress, the irony developing with all of its strength. Pilate believes himself to be the judge, and his prisoner a helpless Jew whom the leaders of his nation seek to force him to execute. The Jewish leaders, following the piety of their formal religious practice, stand without plotting the murder of an innocent man, whose claim (that he is the Messiah) they have rejected. The audience is firmly in their places, observing the events from their position following the resurrection. They, with the author, know the truth. Jesus is the Messiah, the Son of God, who will one day judge Pilate and condemn these Jews who now accuse him. We shall proceed and watch the irony of the drama develop.

Pilate proceeds from his questioning of Jesus to the Jews who are on the outside with a proposition. Pilate will, following the custom of the feast, release Jesus to them because he finds no fault in him. His use of the term "King of the Jews" in his reply seems to show Pilate's understanding. "King" did not have a meaning offensive to him, or to the cause of the Roman Empire he was sent to protect. He can thus feel free to use the term with the Jews and use it contemptuously.[47] Pilate finds Jesus harmless politically, and feels free to release him. The dual accent between what is said and what is meant comes through strongly.

But the Jews do not accept the offer. They cry instead for Barabbas. The irony of their position is cryptically revealed by the author with the addition: "Now Barabbas had taken part in a rebellion" (18:40). It is powerful in its brevity. The word λῃστής used to characterize Barabbas meant that he had committed murder in his revolutionary activities. The irony of the Jews' request is that Barabbas, the convicted murderer, is exactly what makes Jesus worthy of death. Their actions reveal their deceit.[48] Barabbas was what they had accused Jesus of being. They desired his freedom and would send Jesus to his death.

In chapter 19, the irony continues, but in a different vein. The term "King of the Jews" is used in verse 3 by the mocking soldiers, yet the contrast

47. Barrett, *Gospel*, 448–49; Westcott, *Gospel*, 262.
48. Bultmann, *Das Evangelium*, 509.

between the appearance and the reality is made abundantly clear within the larger context. Jesus has been scourged. The soldiers then produce a royal crown made of thorns and a tattered purple robe, and invest them upon Jesus. He is brought forth. The Jews see a pitiful-looking creature, but one who is dressed as a king. Finally, the irony of Pilate's words caps the scene: ἰδοὺ ὁ ἄνθρωπος (19:5). Such a woeful figure of a man is the only king the Jewish leaders are likely to have.

This ironic motif possibly continues in verse 13, where there is a question of whether Jesus or Pilate sits upon the judgment seat. This question seems to have arisen with Harnack's publication of the Gospel of Peter.[49] In this work, as in Justin's Apology 1:35, Jesus is pictured as sitting upon the judgment seat, being mocked by the Jews. The question arises as to whether we should consider the verb "ἐκάθισεν" as transitive or intransitive. The transitive translation would have Pilate place Jesus as judge upon the judgment seat. The intransitive would seat Pilate upon the judgment seat. La Potterie has shown that the grammatical possibility for the transitive translation is strong.[50] He lists three strong arguments: (1) The transitive translation follows the pattern of action of the first part of the verse. Pilate would be the subject, and Jesus the object of both verbs. The action of the transitive verbs would relate to εἰς τόπον. (2) The grammatical pattern of verb, object, second verb, and no second object, with the second transitive verb relying on the object of the first, is common in John. (3) The absence of the definite article with βήματος would indicate that no formal chair of judgment was used, and would thus remove some of the stigma of the scene.

In spite of these arguments and the possible irony that would be conveyed through them, the intransitive translation seems better, as the text reveals a climax in verse 13. Pilate has been pushed to where he must make a decision. The previous mockery of Jesus as a king serves as a tool by which Pilate had hoped to release Jesus (19:6), but this ends in verse 6. Since Pilate has come to "fear more greatly" (v. 8) his prisoner, he questions the true origin of Jesus (v. 9). Thus, it seems unlikely that the author would expect us to revisit the motif of mockery, but the irony in the following passages comes from Pilate's desire to gain revenge against the Jews, not from his desire to mock Jesus as a king. Therefore, the intransitive meaning John uses elsewhere (12:14) is rendered better here.

49. Harnack, *Bruckstücke des Evangeliums*, 51.
50. La Potterie, "Jésus Roi," 231–33.

C. K. Barrett accepts the position of Pilate upon the judgment seat, but would attempt to impose a double meaning upon the text: "We may suppose then that John meant that Pilate did in fact sit upon the βῆμα, but that for those with eyes to see behind this human scene appeared the Son of Man to whom all judgment has been committed (5:22), seated upon his throne."[51] Meeks and La Potterie are wrong when they reject this double meaning on the grounds that double meaning does not come from a grammatical basis.[52] We have demonstrated that the variation in mode is also a basis for double meaning found in the Fourth Gospel.[53] C. K. Barrett's position seems to rest upon the same basis as the intransitive meaning implies. In each case of double meaning, we are dependent upon the author to show us that the double meaning is present, but here he leads us away from such an interpretation. While we cannot deny the truth that the believer might see Jesus sitting on the seat of judgment, judging Pilate and the Jews, and that the ultimate meaning of the passage undoubtedly leads one to this position, only a very strained exegesis can extract it from the text.[54]

With Pilate seated upon the seat of judgment, he proceeds to deliver Jesus to them for crucifixion. Pilate does not say, "This man is being condemned because he claimed to be the king of the Jews." Rather, the very sarcastic words "ἴδε ὁ βασιλεὺς ὑμῶν" (19:14) convey the ironic sense of the scenario, as the cleverness of the Jews to bring Jesus to judgment is brought back as a judgment upon them. "The helpless prisoner of Rome is the only king they are likely to have."[55]

The most tragic irony of the whole passage now bursts upon us. To Pilate's question, "Shall I crucify your king?", the high priests rise to answer, "We have no king but Caesar!" (v. 15). How far this is from the monotheistic tradition of Israel! God was their king (Ps 10:16; 24:8–10; 44:4; and the hymn sung at the conclusion of the Greater Hallel).[56] While the Jews undoubtedly intended their statement to carry only political connotations, one cannot help but consider the deeper religious connotations the author

51. Barrett, *Gospel*, 453.

52. Meeks, *Prophet King*, 74; La Potterie, "Jésus Roi," 218n2.

53. Note chiefly pp. 64–66 above.

54. The key to the line between irony and double meaning seems to be the ability of the author to show us that he intends double meaning. Here we find no such intention in the context of the passage. Double meaning seems to demand that both aspects of the meaning be true. Irony involves a contradiction, and is therefore not double meaning.

55. Barrett, *Gospel*, 454.

56. Meeks, *Prophet King*, 77.

saw within it. They were rejecting their true messianic king, who was sent from God, and the religious implications are inextricably bound with it.[57] By their rejection of the salvation of the Lord, the Jewish leaders have destroyed that which it was their purpose to save: the place of their nation with the Romans (11:48), but even more so with God.[58] The doom of Israel is sealed, as their leaders have rejected their place as the chosen people of God.

Pilate's reaction to the pressure of the Jews is not yet complete. He can once more employ the title of "the King of the Jews," to their consternation. The "titulus" is thus erected upon the cross, "Jesus of Nazareth, the King of the Jews." The sarcasm is so great that the Jews complain, asking to have it changed, but to no avail. Thus Pilate (as did Caiaphas[59]) unwittingly utters a dictum that believers understand to be profoundly true.[60]

Thus, we can see the depth of the irony the author wished to convey. In truth, the reality was nearly the opposite of that which appeared to those participating in the action. The accused was in reality the king and judge, and the ruler and the accusers were ironically the ones being judged. The Jewish leaders had gained a victory over Pilate, but they lost that for which they hoped. They had denied their Messiah,[61] who in the end is hailed as their king. The consequences of their rejection of the Messiah is that they committed their nation to a path outside God's will. They lost what hope they might have had.

The Origin of the Christ

The accounts of the birth of Christ are strikingly missing from the Gospel of John. This should not be interpreted to mean that scholars do not find references to such (note 1:13, especially) or that we consider that all references to the birth of Christ are found in passages that ought to be interpreted ironically. We cannot assume with Renan and others from the omission of accounts of the birth that John rejected the birth traditions as untrue. In John, the emphasis lies not on the birth of Jesus, but rather on the origin of Jesus. It is not nearly so important that Jesus was born in Bethlehem of a

57. Meeks, *Prophet King*, 64.

58. Haenchen, "Jesus vor Pilatus," 98.

59. Barrett, *Gospel*, 457.

60. Bultmann, *Das Evangelium*, 518.

61. Schlier, "Jesus und Pilatus," 73.

virgin who belonged to the seed of David, as it was that he was the Son of God (μονογενής), who was with God from the beginning.

The technique of the unanswered question becomes a characteristic style the author uses to make his irony felt.[62] We have noted above the author's ability to employ such a technique in 6:52.[63] With regard to the origin of Jesus, such a technique is used in four places (6:42; 7:42; 8:19; 19:9). Such an extensive use leads us away from assuming that the author leaves questions unanswered because he did not know the answer or that he accepted the "no" implied by the μή as the correct answer. Assuming that the author presents the life of Jesus so that audiences might believe Jesus was the Christ, the Son of God (20:31), it is unbelievable to think that he would call attention to so many obvious holes in his own argument. Rather, he was relying on the fact that the Gospel's readers, either through contact with the Synoptics or through other traditions of the Christ, would have the knowledge to supply the answers to the questions. Here again, the elements necessary for irony come clearly before us. The relationship of the author to the main character and his assumption about the knowledge of the audience allow the evangelist to proceed in this fashion.[64]

When addressing the oddities of the following passages, a number of elements lead us to believe that the author was treating the theme ironically. The most important is the number of passages where irony is apparent. A strong case would be hard to build if there were only one or two verses to support an inference, but several instances allow the device of irony to be seen from different angles. The number of times John turns to the question of Jesus' birth leads us to see the author's intent, as they also bear witness to one another and should be considered as a whole.

The thrust of John's use of irony related to the birth of the Christ is best understood by looking into the evangelist's references to views of messianic origins current within his first-century setting. In John 7, the evangelist gives us a glimpse into the Jewish expectation of the coming of their Messiah. The first is the theory of the unknown origin of the Messiah.[65] The argument of the people is that Jesus cannot be the Christ because "we know where this man is from; when the Christ comes, no one will know where he is from" (7:27). This presupposes their understanding that Jesus

62. Barrett, *Gospel*, 251.

63. See p. 10.

64. Salmon, *Historical Introduction*, 276–78.

65. Dodd, *Interpretation*, 89.

was born in Galilee because he was raised there. The reader is to consider the inference ironically, knowing that it is wrong, and C. H. Dodd is helpful when he notes that

> Jesus is made to admit that the Jews know His origin, but, with an irony characteristic of this gospel, a hint is given to the reader that His true origin is even more mysterious and august than that of the hidden Messiah of Jewish expectation; He comes, not from Rome or the north, or from any unknown place of concealment, but direct from God Himself.[66]

The intent of the argument thus shows us that Jesus is not really from Galilee, but from God. Therefore, the Jews did not really know where Jesus came from, and he thus could indeed be the hidden Messiah.

The second view is related to the facts concerning the birth of Jesus given in Matthew and Luke. The people question in verse 42: "Does not the Scripture say that the Christ will come from David's family and from Bethlehem, the town where David lived?" They imply by their unanswered question that Jesus cannot be the Christ because he was born in Galilee. Again, the author implies they are wrong, and the movement of the argument depends upon it.

> On the basis of the parallelism between 27 and 42, then, we believe that the evangelist knew perfectly well of the tradition that Jesus was born at Bethlehem. Since he expected that this tradition would be known by his readers, this mistake of the Jews in vs. 42 would be apparent to them, even as was the mistake in 27.[67]

These first two passages seem to work against Meeks' theory of Galilean origin.[68] In both, the ironic answer demands the truth that Jesus was not really born in Galilee. The irony is present because the author does not want us to consider that the ultimate answer was Bethlehem. The more important fact is that Jesus had his origin in heaven with God.[69]

The third view of the origin of the Messiah deals with the rise of the apocalyptic prophet. "Are you from Galilee, too? Look into it, and you will find that a prophet does not come out of Galilee" (7:52). As long ago

---

66. Dodd, *Interpretation*, 89.

67. Brown, *Gospel According to John (i–xii)*, 330.

68. Meeks, *Prophet King*, 36–41.

69. Bernard, *Critical and Exegetical Commentary*, 286; Barrett, *Gospel*, 272–73; Brown, *Gospel According to John (i–xii)*, lxxiv.

as 1903, Carr pointed out in the *Expositor* that the definite article in this passage should point not to any prophet, but to a distinctive prophet. The recently published Bodmer papyri support Carr with their testimony to the correctness of the definite article.[70] Yet most have followed the interpretation that this refers to the Old Testament prophets, an interpretation that leads to the dilemma: Old Testament prophets, most notably Jonah, did arise out of Galilee. With the coming of the archeological discoveries of Qumran, we have found references also to this strain of messianic interpretation (1QS 9:11; 4QTest 5—8). "The" prophet had come to be considered an apocalyptic figure. Discussion remains as to whether such a figure was the proposed Messiah or a separate figure.[71]

The emphasis again is upon the fact that, although Jesus appeared to arise out of Galilee, this was not really the case. Thus, the evangelist is arguing between the "appearance" of what the people observed and the "realty" the author and his readers know to be true. In all cases, the supposed Galilean origin of Jesus is thus a false supposition of the people. The argument that Jesus is the Messiah proceeds on the fact that the Jewish reasoning is right, but that their concept is governed by appearance, and the true realty is not a part of their knowledge. They do not know where he came from, as they think of him as coming only from Galilee and not from God. Thus, Jesus fulfills the role of the traditions and prophecies as one of unknown origin, and so he is the Christ.

In two further passages, the author develops a different aspect of the problem of the origin of Jesus: the illegitimacy of the birth of Jesus.[72] Here, John builds his irony around a theme current in Jewish circles, and again, the passages gain strength by their number. The ironic references are found both in chapters 6 and 8.

In chapter 6, the passage comes in the middle of the discourse on the Bread of Life. The setting is Galilean, and the audience is acquainted with the accounts of Jesus' family having come from Nazareth. Jesus has told them that he is the bread coming down from heaven, but they understand this as a claim that he has a heavenly origin. They thus object to this claim, because they know his mother and his supposed father. After all, Joseph has raised him to work in the carpenter's shop (v. 42): "Is this not Jesus, the son

---

70. Metzger, *Text*, 48; Carr, "Note on St. John," 219–26.

71. Woude, *Die Messianischen Vorstellungen*, 75–88; Schnackenburg, "Die Erwartung," 622–39; Jeremias, "Μωϋσῆς," 862; Cullmann, *Die Christologie*, 11.

72. Brown, *Gospel According to John (i–xii)*, 357.

of Joseph?" John leaves their question, but has Jesus go on with his teaching on the Bread of Life. The question asked in the discourse can only have one answer: if Jesus had come from heaven, the Jews did not know his true Father. Their argument is that one whose local parentage is known cannot have come down from heaven.

Even though the evangelist is content to let stand the reference to the fact that Jesus is the son of Joseph (1:45), there can be little doubt that he did not consider this more than a formal mode of identification of the earthly situation in which Jesus lived.[73] The contrast the author wishes to draw between the reality and the appearance of the situation again rests upon the assumed doctrine of the virgin birth. He is willing to let the contrast between reality and appearance stand with the confidence that the audience is of one mind with him and knows the thrust of the case.[74]

[handwritten margin note: Leap to virgin birth]

The author brings us another unanswered question to begin our exploration in 8:19, where the following question arises: ποῦ ἐστιν ὁ πατήρ σου? Jesus does not answer their question directly, but goes on to show them that they do not know his Father. They are undoubtedly referring to his earthly father, but do they really consider Joseph his father, or are they following the rumor that Jesus was conceived out of wedlock? We believe the latter. Not only does this fit the ironic method of the author, but it also follows the train of thought evident in the answer of Jesus. He avoids any attempt to tell the audience that Jesus' father was Joseph. (He also does not and cannot give the answer the author and his readers know to be true: God.) Jesus asserts that the Jews do not know his father because they do not really know his origin. This points us away from Joseph as the answer the Jews expected, and it allows us to wonder if the illegitimacy of Jesus' birth was not already popularly current and being used by those who opposed him.

In verse 41 we find another ironic reference to the illegitimate birth of Jesus. "'We are not illegitimate children,' they protested, 'The only Father we have is God himself'"; "The Jews find a fresh way of turning the argument against Jesus. The implication (especially of the emphatic ἡμεῖς) is that Jesus was born of πορνείας."[75] He is willing to let the contrast stand between reality and appearance with the confidence that the audience is of one mind with him and knows the truth.

73. Bernard, *Critical and Exegetical Commentary*, 62; Barrett, *Gospel*, 153.

74. Barrett, *Gospel*, 280; Hoskyns, *Fourth Gospel*, 322–23.

75. Lampe and Woollcombe, *Essays on Typology*, 22.

All of these statements about the Johannine handling of the birth of Jesus point us to these last ones. They bear the true intent of the author. He does not wish us to be content with the belief that Jesus was born in Bethlehem, or the discussions about the fatherhood of Joseph, or the illegitimacy of Jesus' birth. He wished to ultimately point us to the truth that lies behind the discussion, and which must reign supreme: Jesus is of heavenly origin. Both his Father and his place of origin are heavenly.

An exploration of πόθεν in the Gospel of John thus points us to the heavenly origin of the Christ. In 8:14, John states: "Jesus answered, 'Even if I testify on my own behalf, my testimony is valid, for I know where I came from and where I am going.'" The reader cannot miss the heavenly reference of the statement (1:17), as we have already noted the ironic use of πόθεν ἐστίν in 7:27. The Jews claim that they know where Jesus has come from, but in truth, they do not.

The exact opposite is stated in 9:29: "We know that God spoke to Moses, but as for this fellow, we do not even where he comes from [πόθεν ἐστίν]." Raymond E. Brown sees this verse as another hint of the illegitimate birth of Jesus.[76] By now, the author is sure that the audience will understand the importance of the phrase; Jesus is greater than Moses. The true answer is that Jesus has come from God, and the irony of this statement lies in the contrast between the appearance and the reality of the situation. They had stated earlier (7:27) that one of the marks of messiahship was that his origin would be unknown, and yet here they ironically reject his messianic role for this very reason.[77]

The culmination of this irony comes before us in 19:9, where in the trial scene we find this unanswered question: πόθεν εἶ σύ? The author emphasizes the silence of Jesus in response to it. Pilate has no answer, and is only left to suppose; but the reader indeed knows the anwer.[78] And by this time, the questioned province of Jesus' birth is answered easily in the mind of the reader: he must be "from above." His origin is thus both known and unknown.[79]

76. Brown, *Gospel According to John (i–xii)*, 356.

77. Barrett, *Gospel*, 301.

78. Hoskyns, *Fourth Gospel*, 523; Mollat and Braun, *L'Évangile*, 180.

79. Barrett, *Gospel*, 451.

The Superiority of Jesus to the Patriarchs

This third category follows the same pattern as the second, implied mostly through questions that are unanswered. The people of the land, both Jews and Samaritans, held high esteem for the patriarchs, as these venerated men represented the covenants and the promises of God. Thus, for the people of that day, no one surpassed the patriarchs. Yet John and his readers know this is no longer the case. Not only is Jesus greater than the patriarchs, but the promises that have been left in his covenant are of greater value than those left by the patriarchs.[80]

In the fourth chapter, the Samaritan woman does not realize she is speaking to the Messiah. She is preoccupied with material water, while Jesus speaks to her of spiritual water. In verse 12, the irony of the situation comes to a head, with the unanswered question playing an important role: "Are you greater than our father Jacob who gave us the well and drank from it himself, as did also his sons and his flocks and herds?" The μή introducing the sentence shows the answer she expects.[81] Her reasoning leads her to suppose that Jacob is greater than Jesus, but John and his readers know the woman is wrong, and the woman soon understands her error, too (4:29). Jacob had taken care to provide for bodily needs and the needs of their cattle, but the Christ would provide for her spiritual needs unto the ages.[82]

The same question is repeated word for word in 8:53, with one exception: the patriarch Jacob is exchanged for the patriarch Abraham. The Jews suppose that Jesus is inferior to their great patriarch, Abraham, and the prophets are now also added to the consideration. However, they and Abraham have died, and Jesus now claims that those who keep his word shall not see death. Does he think he is greater than the patriarchs?

The discussion continues (with the question again unanswered) turning to the source of the glory Christ receives. In verse 56, the subject turns to Abraham once more. Again, we note the irony of the question that the Jews put forth: "'You are not yet fifty years old,' the Jews said to him, 'and you have seen Abraham!'" (v. 57). They see a man who is obviously not old (fifty years), who claims to have been seen by the ancient patriarch. They cannot realize the fact known to John and his readers: Jesus is the Logos of God, who has existed from the beginning. In this passage, which ends the

---

80. Lightfoot, *St. John's Gospel*, 134.

81. Blass et al., *Greek Grammar*, §427, 220–21; cf. also Westcott, *Gospel*, 70.

82. Büchsel, *Das Evangelium*, 63.

irony of the theme, John shows Jesus leaving no one in doubt as to what he claims: "I tell you the truth," Jesus answered, "Before Abraham was, I am" (ἐγὼ εἰμί). John and his readers know that Jesus is greater than Abraham because he is the only begotten Son of God.[83]

The Destruction of the Temple

This theme that forms a definite part of the Passion Week in the synoptic accounts (Matt 26:61; Mark 14:58) also comes in the Gospel of John, but in a very different context.[84] The Johannine account may provide the basis for the charges the Synoptics bring before us.

The ironic handling of the theme is evident in John 11:48: "If we let him go on like this, everyone will believe in him and then the Romans will come and take away both our temple [τόπος] and our nation." While τόπος may refer either to the city of Jerusalem or the temple, the strength of other New Testament usage (cf. Acts 6:13) and Rabbinic sources points us to the temple rendering.[85] The ironic fact about the whole verse is that the Jews accomplished just exactly what they sought to avoid by the crucifixion of Jesus. They had hoped to stop the flow of people who were believing in him by putting him to death. At the time of the writing of the Gospel, this flow had not stopped, but had increased, so that it was now spreading throughout the entire world.

However, the irony goes deeper, because by the time the Gospel had been written, the Romans had also come and destroyed the temple, and the Jewish nation was about to be scattered. The Jewish leaders had accomplished what they attempted to avoid through their rejection and crucifixion of Jesus. Here and in 2:19–22, the author connects the crucifixion of Jesus with the removal of the Jewish nation from God's favor. As the rejection of their king actually expressed their rejection of God and God's Son as their king, so here the crucifixion resulted in the dissolution of their relation with God. It sealed the destruction of the temple.

We see this fact reinforced in 2:19–22, where the concept of irony and double meaning are conjoined. We have deferred the discussion of these verses until now so we can bring both concepts—irony and double

83. Dodd, *Interpretation*, 251.

84. Brown, *Gospel According to John (i–xii)*, 442.

85. Winter, *On the Trial of Jesus*, 40, argues that τόπος should refer to the position of authority the Sanhedrin held.

meaning—to bear upon them. Jesus declares in 2:19: "Destroy this temple and I will raise it again in three days." The irony of the passage is couched in the first clause of the sentence. This part of the sentence is more than a simple condition, but is an ironic imperative as the prophets of the Old Testament used (Amos 4:4; Isa 8:9).[86] Bultmann notes that this first clause, the prophetic statement, follows a characteristic form. Jesus is implying that the destruction will be the result of Jewish unbelief. The eschatological salvation is represented in the new temple, which is the completion of his messianic mission.[87] Thus, Jesus tells the Jews that they shall destroy what they treasure, the holy temple. The reference to the temple is required by the context. One should not expect that Jesus would completely omit the reference to the temple in the saying; when he used the word, he was in the building, and he was questioned just after cleansing it.

Thus, in explaining that "the temple he had spoken of was his body" (v. 21), the author is not turning us completely away from the reference to the temple, but rather to the double meaning he intended.[88] When one compares the Johannine expression of the saying with that recorded in the Synoptics, one must note a striking change in the key terms. Καταλύω in the Synoptics becomes λύω in John, and οἰκοδομέω becomes ἐγείρω. In each case, the synoptic terms are applicable to the destruction of the building and its rebuilding, but they are not applicable to the death and return to life of the human body.[89] The Johannine terms are seemingly chosen with specificity because they are so applicable.[90]

Thus, in light of the reference in 11:48 and the reasons listed above, we believe the author intended a double meaning here. We should like to propose that Jesus meant this through the double meaning: "Destroy this body [in which I live] and you shall destroy also this temple [in which we stand], and I shall raise up a new temple to take its place in a short time." Such an interpretation would apply the double meaning only to the first part of the statement, so it seems impossible to apply it to the latter part. Not only does the statement of the Jews show the author's understanding that we should not look for another temple made with hands to appear (v.

---

86. Dodd, *Interpretation*, 302n1, is probably wrong when he traces this usage back to the simple conditional usage we would find in the Semitic background.

87. Bultmann, *Das Evangelium*, 88.

88. Bultmann, *Das Evangelium*, 88.

89. Bauer, *Greek-English Lexicon*.

90. Hoskyns, *Fourth Gospel*, 194–95.

20), but there is also no indication from history that this has happened. Certainly, the "short time" the text denotes could not have been extended beyond the author's lifetime.

The Jews expected that the Messiah should build a temple, and the Dead Sea Scrolls are clear in stating the Messiah will come bringing a new temple. However, here the Johannine community is considered as the new temple, even as the church is regarded as the new Israel elsewhere in the New Testament.[91] The replacement of the temple with the church infers the body of Christ, which offers forgiveness on the basis of Christ's sacrifice, through the death of his body.[92] The Jewish Christ now becomes the new temple, replacing that which the Jews destroyed ironically by their misguided attempts to save it. In their attempt to save their holy place, they crucified him who would bring fulfillment to it.

The Irony Related to Discipleship

The final theme is not as unified, as the ones previously discussed. We cannot pick one running theme around which the irony is built. Yet what we can see in a number of passages in which the function of irony is observable as a tool employed subtly by the author to spur some readers to come to embrace faith in Jesus as the Christ for the first time, and to inspire believers to deeper commitments of faithfulness (20:30–31).

As John 7:48–52 illustrates the various ways the author might approach the subject of irony, we earlier noted that the Jewish leaders were unaware that Nicodemus or any others had come to faith. The irony of the passage thus implies that some of the Jewish rulers had come secretly to faith, and that the teachings of Jesus had even affected those in positions of leadership.

We may note also such an ironic call to faith: "If you believed Moses, you would believe me, for he wrote about me. But since you do not believe what he wrote, how are you going to believe what I say?" (5:46–47). There was no one whom the Jewish leaders held in higher regard than Moses, and there was nothing that they studied more than the law. Thus, it would be easy for Jewish members of John's audience to assert that this claim was not true; yet the Johannine believer knows that it is. As Moses predicted that God would raise up a prophet like him, who would speak faithfully

91. 1QS 5.5–7; 8.7–10; 1QH 6.25–28; see, for instance, Romans 9–11.

92. Schlatter, *Der Evangelist Johannes*, 79.

on God's behalf (Deut 18:15–22), the Jews ironically did not connect Jesus with the fulfillment of that prophecy. Thus, we are left with the concluding question we noted above, and the question is unanswered, following the pattern of the author. This would stand not only as the concluding statement in the discourse of Jesus, but also as a continuing call to faith for all who valued the law of Moses.

The irony in John 7:33–34 leads us into the same line of thought. Jesus says, "I am with you for only a short time, and then I go to the one who sent me. You will look for me, but you will not find me; and where I am you cannot come." Ironically, the Jews would seek their Messiah, but only after he had returned to the Father. But then it would be too late; they would seek him and not be able to find him.[93] The author and his readers can review the events of history to see that such Messianic expectations had led to the destruction of Jerusalem and the temple, and future events would lead to even greater conflagrations under Bar Kokhba. Yet all their seeking would be in vain, and later readers would appreciate the ironic rejection of the true Messiah, who Moses predicted, by those claiming to be his most devout followers.

John 9, in which the blind man is healed, is also replete with irony. Throughout the chapter, the irony is made stronger because the ignorant blind man becomes the teacher of those Pharisees who, by their rank and education, should have been his teacher (note especially 9:30–31).[94] The irony reaches a climax in verse 27 with an unanswered question: "I have told you already and you did not listen. Why do you want to hear it again? Do you want to become his disciples, too?" This is undoubtedly the μή of cautious assertion.[95] The blind man hopes that the Pharisees may become disciples of Christ, but ironically his hopes are unfulfilled. The Pharisees have already made up their minds that they should not become disciples of Jesus, but were attempting to force the former blind man into a denial of his newfound faith.

Finally, Jesus and the Pharisees come face to face, and the blind man fades into the background. This time, the Pharisees ask the ironic question: "What? Are we blind too?" (9:40). The μή shows that they expect to be

---

93. Barrett, *Gospel*, 268; Bultmann, *Das Evangelium*, 232; Hoskyns, *Fourth Gospel*, 319; Westcott, *Gospel*, 122.

94. Dodd, *Interpretation*, 357–58.

95. Blass et al., *Greek Grammar*, §220–21; Moulton, *Grammar*, 192–93; Barrett, *Gospel*, 300.

told they are blind, and that they must have been surprised and stunned by the answer. Their claim to sight condemns them to responsibility for their ignorance. They are not totally blind. They are willfully blind—to the extent that they can be called blind—and the play on the double aspects of physical and spiritual blindness falls upon them with full force. They claim to see both physically and spiritually, and thus they are condemned. Their claim to a little sight is that which condemns them: "No, you are not wholly blind; that is the worst feature of your case."[96]

In conclusion, we should emphasize that the irony of John is largely present at the choice of the author. "I believe that in that Gospel can be found as many cases as in all the rest of the New Testament, where the characters are introduced as speaking under misapprehensions the reader knows how to correct."[97] Thus we can see the irony, not so much in the words of Jesus as in the entire setting and the words of the other characters in the divine drama. Jesus, like the evangelist, had a divine insight into the entire meaning of the situation. Therefore, he does not only see the appearance of things, or that which those who are limited to the perception of their senses in a given moment of time experience, but he also discerns the true reality of the situation, or that which is the true impact of the event in its relation to all of history. The irony here is thus much more Sophoclean than Socratic.

The unanswered question—a characteristic of the Johannine irony—shows that the author depended on the ability of the audience to answer such questions. Because the appearance of the characters is limited to the earthly side of most questions, the author is prone to follow the classical pattern of irony and understate one's case. The reader is then left to grasp the full and true meaning of the complete situation that the author has implied by the use of irony.

The themes gain their true importance by divine insight into the true reality of the life of Jesus. John acts upon the assumption that his readers have superior knowledge from his prologue, the information he has given to begin the Gospel, and other traditions known to Christians. This superior knowledge forms the basis for the reality upon which irony depends. The author develops the themes ironically so that their truth is strengthened. By his repeated reference to these themes, he reinforces them so we can gain certainty regarding the use of irony. Throughout the Gospel, the

96. Bernard, *Critical and Exegetical Commentary*, 341.
97. Salmon, *Historical Introduction*, 281.

divine spiritual reality thus remains clearly before our eyes, bolstered by this powerful literary device.

Excursus into the Misunderstandings

One might ask why an attempt to explore the literary devices of the writer of the Fourth Gospel would not take up the question of the prevalent misunderstandings. Our omission of this heading does not indicate our having failed to recognize its importance, but rather an inability to categorize it in exclusion to the other categories. In each of the last three chapters, the author has used misunderstanding as a means to present his case.

Such misunderstandings often take the form of the unanswered question, which we found so prevalent in the chapter on irony. Blunt misunderstanding in the form of a direct statement is also presented by the author, revealing a character's misapprehension when engaged with the words of Jesus. As Barrett puts it,

> Such misunderstandings are very characteristic of John and are often, as here, more than a literary trick employed by a writer given to irony. They represent in miniature the total reaction of Judaism to Christ; the Jews perceived only what was superficially visible in Jesus and naturally reflected as absurd the suggestion that he should be the Son of God; if they had penetrated beneath the surface they would have seen the truth.[98]

The misapprehension is usually based upon the inability of the earthly character to grasp any more than a mere earthly truth (8:23).

This misunderstanding becomes an opportunity for the author to advance or emphasize his case. In the double meaning, the author could use such a situation to bring out the true meaning of the double meaning word (3:3). The misunderstanding of the woman at the well became the ironical basis upon which the discussion continued (4:12). In both cases, the author takes the occasion to define more clearly the meaning of Jesus that he wished to convey to his readers.

We have seen the misunderstanding in connection with each of these two chapters because each of them, in its own way, deals with more than one aspect of the meaning of the situation. When dealing with the sign, we found that the events which took place pointed to the person and ministry

98. Barrett, *Gospel*, 166.

of Jesus. As this miraculous feeding is related to the person of Jesus, the misunderstanding of the Jews arises: "How can this man give us his flesh to eat?" (6:52). When dealing with the double meaning, Nicodemus cannot understand how a man can be born again (3:4). Thus, Jesus brings out the double meaning of the passage involved. The irony of the passages dealing with the kingship of Jesus emphasized the failure of the characters to note more than the earthly aspect (appearance) of the events in which they were involved. The divine meaning (the spiritual reality) is beyond their comprehension, and thus the irony develops.

In each case, the person involved may be either partially or completely wrong. He or she may miss the point of the word altogether, as the woman at the well (4:12), or may come to grasp with only one aspect, as we usually find in irony or with Nicodemus. In each case, the author needed to be able to define more clearly what Jesus meant.

Thus, while the technique of misunderstanding is one peculiar to the author of the Fourth Gospel, we believe that we should also recognize that such a technique is not truly a literary device, but merely a technique by which the more precise meanings and the other literary devices of the author are revealed more clearly to his readers.

CHAPTER 5

THE JOHANNINE METAPHORS

The word μεταφωρά was a part of the Greek language as early as Homer, who used the word to describe the modern metaphor, as well as the simile. One of the earliest definitions we find is that of Aristotle: "Metaphor is the transference of a strange name either from a kind to an image or from an image to a kind or from an image to an image or according to analogy."[1] This definition does not deal with the meaning involved, as much as with the formation of the metaphor. The rhetorical nature of his work aided functional formation. It did not seek to explain the semantics. This we must seek to do.

The first and only break from this functional definition before the modern period comes with Hermogenes of Tarsus (ca. 170 CE). He defines metaphor as follows: "It is oblique language when a term not relevant to the subject matter but signifying some extraneous object of reference is introduced into the sentence so as to unite its significance in both the subject at issue and the extraneous object of reference in a composite concept."[2] To do this clearly involves a change of meaning. This definition redirects our attention from how to make the metaphor to what happens when we use one. This union of concepts has brought forth new definitions/meanings of words throughout the history of language.

THE DEFINITION OF THE METAPHOR

The metaphor properly moves into the area of figurative speech.[3] We cannot create the concept according to the literal meanings, so we must apply

1. Aristotle, *Poetics*, 21.4 (translated by W. H. Fyfe).
2. As quoted in Stanford, *Greek Metaphor*, 8.
3. Jülicher, *Die Gleichnisse Jesu*, 52.

a figurative meaning to them.[4] When we are placed in a situation where we cannot apply the literal meaning, then we are forced to apply that which is figurative. It is not reasonable to believe that a man is a lion. Therefore, we must interpret this word figuratively as a metaphor.

Change of meaning is vital to the metaphor.[5] Metaphor is the result of a union of terms, elements chosen because of their importance to express a new relationship. These elements of meaning thus unite to produce new meanings. A new meaning may be assumed later by one of the terms, but in the original formation of the metaphor, it is the union of terms into one word that produces a new meaning. The terms therefore lose their original meanings within their new contexts.[6]

More than one element goes into the new meaning. It includes shades from the entire concept. The metaphor does not merely imply that characteristics from A and B are brought together, although certain characteristics will naturally be more important than others, but that the basic concepts as a whole will enter the combination. This new relationship that evolves cannot be denoted by A-B, because it is usual that new ideas and concepts result form a unique combination of the two ideas. Imagination becomes an important part of any metaphorical union because metaphors are intended to express new thoughts. In short, metaphors often create new meanings.[7]

Thus, the definition as given by Stanford seems adequate. It emphasizes the union of both elements, along with the new aspects of meaning that develop.

> The term metaphor is fully valid only applied to a very definite and rather complicated concept, viz. the process and result of using a term (X) normally signifying an object or concept (A) in such a context that it must refer to another object or concept (B) which is distinct enough in characteristics from A to ensure that in the composite idea formed by the syntheses of the concepts A & B are now symbolized in the word X, the factors A & B retain their conceptual independence even while they merge in the unity symbolized by X.[8]

---

4. Konrad, *Étude sur la Métaphore*, 27.

5. Konrad, *Étude sur la Métaphore*, 28.

6. Stern, *Meaning*, 305.

7. Stern, *Meaning*, 308; cf. also Stanford, *Greek Metaphor*, 100.

8. Stanford, *Greek Metaphor*, 101.

The importance of the new unity, symbolized by "X," points us to the change of meaning that must take place for the metaphor to function properly.

In our evaluation of the metaphorical expression, we cannot separate the terms or even hope to analyze the characteristics that might make up the metaphor. "One can no more prophesy probable meaning from a word's form than one can deduce a man's personality from an anatomical study of the body."[9] Metaphor must be considered as a part of a complete picture (words and contexts) that comes before the minds of the hearers.

Thus, we have a definite process of thought that must take place when we come in contact with a metaphor. This process of thought leads us from the literal meanings of the words and then to a figurative meaning, and then further to the new meanings that result from the union of concepts.

The camel is the ship of the desert. We know exactly what a ship is: it is a vehicle that carries people and cargo on the sea. It has certain characteristics, such as wood or steel construction, and it moves at certain speeds and is steered in certain manner. These are not, however, qualities of a camel. Rather, we picture a large animal with special abilities to endure heat and to function well with little water. The camel has very different qualities from a ship. The metaphor calls us to seek out characteristics related to a ship, e.g., the ability to carry cargo or people, and to do this in a very different environment than the ship, e.g., in hot lands.[10]

Not only does this illustration point out the different spheres of meaning for the concepts involved in the metaphor, but it also directs us to the impossibility of considering the concepts involved in their literal spheres. Thus, we are forced into searching for the change of meaning involved.

This should draw our attention to the difference between the metaphor and the simile. The metaphor is more than just a shortened simile.[11] In form, the simile carries a comparative particle not found with the metaphor, but the differences go much deeper than this. Because the simile compares, it is literal speech. We have seen that the metaphor is figurative.[12] The comparative nature of the simile is different from the metaphor in that it holds the elements of the two forms separate while drawing a comparison

---

9. Stanford, *Greek Metaphor*, 82.

10. Stählin, *Zur Psychologie*, 26.

11. Against Bultmann, *Die Geschichte*, 183, and Schweizer, *Ego Eimi*, 113–14; but following Jülicher, *Die Gleichnisse Jesu*, 53; Stählin, *Zur Psychologie*, 43–44, and Stern, *Meaning*, 308.

12. Jülicher, *Die Gleichnisse Jesu*, 54.

between them. The function of the metaphor is different in that it unites the forms. The mode of making the inferences that are drawn from the figures is also different. When an author uses a simile, one draws the comparison for one's hearers. When using a metaphor, the author depends upon his or her audience to make the inference that results in the new meaning.[13]

Double meaning differs from the metaphor in that the double meaning would hold separate the two aspects of meaning. No new meaning or change of meaning is involved in the double meaning. There is no union of concepts. Double meaning only accepts the processes of language that have developed, largely through the metaphorical usages, and it makes use of these developments. Metaphorical usage develops new meanings, and it does not rely on what has gone before. The double meaning, however, has no such pioneering spirit.

This metaphorical process may also lie behind the formation of symbols, which are images that have come to represent concepts. Toelken shows that, in many early English ballads, symbols were regularly used again and again. There was a definite connection between the gathering of nuts, or the picking of a rose, and the loss of a girl's virginity.[14] But again, these symbols do not participate in a change of meaning, but are only used when an object—possibly as a result of a common metaphor—is so thoroughly associated with a concept that the object can represent it without the metaphorical usage. The symbol is only possible when we arrive at the final step of the metaphorical process, and such a process has solidified into the place where the word can become a token for the second idea.

THE JOHANNINE METAPHOR

While many types of metaphors are used in the Gospel of John, the most noted are the images and terms associated with the "I am" passages. The question, therefore, is how to interpret these references, and along these lines leading scholars may disagree. Interpretation may receive an assist from considering the use of metaphors in Matthew's Gospel, although a closer look at how they are used in John will be the most telling.

13. Stern, *Meaning*, 304, 337.
14. Toelken, "Oral Canon," 75–102.

The "I Am" Passages

When one turns to the metaphorical uses found in the Gospel of John, the first and most important to be considered are the "I am" passages. These passages are important to any study of John, for they cover the majority of the important concepts and the essential proclamations of the messianic role of the Christ found in the Gospel. The ἐγώ εἰμι formula appears in the Fourth Gospel in the following places:

    4:26—ἐγώ εἰμι, ὁ λαλῶν
    6:35, 48—ἐγώ εἰμι ὁ ἄρτος τῆς ζωῆς
    6:41—ἐγώ εἰμι ὁ ἄρτος ὁ καταβὰς ἐκ τοῦ οὐρανου
    6:51—ἐγώ εἰμι ὁ ἄρτος ὁ ζῶν ὁ ἐκ τοῦ οὐρανοῦ καταβάς
    8:12—ἐγώ εἰμι τὸ φῶς τοῦ κόσμου
    8:18—ἐγώ εἰμι ὁ μαρτυρῶν περὶ ἐμαυτοῦ
    8:23—ἐγὼ οὐκ εἰμὶ ἐκ τοῦ κόσμου τούτου
    9:5—φῶς εἰμι τοῦ κόσμου
    10:7—ἐγώ εἰμι ἡ θύρα τῶν προβάτων
    10:9—ἐγώ εἰμι ἡ θύρα
    10:11, 14—Ἐγώ εἰμι ὁ ποιμὴν ὁ καλός
    11:25—ἐγώ εἰμι ἡ ἀνάστασις καὶ ἡ ζωή
    14:6—ἐγώ εἰμι ἡ ὁδὸς καὶ ἡ ἀλήθεια καὶ ἡ ζωή
    15:1—Ἐγώ εἰμι ἡ ἄμπελος ἡ ἀληθινὴ
    15:5—ἐγώ εἰμι ἡ ἄμπελος

We would make the following preliminary observations on these passages:

1. In 4:26 and 8:18, the structure immediately calls attention to their difference. In 8:23, ἐγὼ οὐκ εἰμὶ means "I am not from." The difference in structure shows us that the author intended them to be interpreted literally and disjunctively. Thus, for the purposes of our examination, these statements can be eliminated. They are not metaphorical.

2. Each of the remaining passages, with the exception of 9:5, is formed in the following pattern: (a) ἐγὼ, (b) εἰμὶ, (c) the definite article with an accompanying noun, (d) the noun may be followed by a genitive (6:35, 48; 8:12; 9:5; 10:7); an adjective (10:11, 14; 15:5); a participle (6:41, 51); other nouns (11:25; 14:6); or by nothing at all (10:9; 15:1).

3. Of these seven different expressions used with "I am," five are repeated twice or more. Of these five, only one always appears in the same form: "ὁ ποιμὴν ὁ καλός." Another, "ὁ ἄρτος τῆς ζωῆς," appears twice in the same form and twice with a different form. A third, "τὸ φῶς τοῦ

κόσμου," uses the light of the world in the second case, but is lacking the ἐγὼ and the definite article. The order of the sentence also endures some changes.

4. These figures, which form the second part of the sentences, have a background in the Palestinian milieu, without exception.[15] But in each case, the background cannot completely provide the full picture we find in the form. Thus, we must look elsewhere for the completion.

5. In each case, the statement of the figure does not stand alone, but is further expressed either by a discourse, a sign, or both. Thus, we find the feeding of the five thousand (6:5–13) and the discourse of the bread of life. The healing of the man born blind (9:6–8) is connected to the statements on the light of the world (9:5) by ταῦτα εἰπὼν. The resulting discussion between the Pharisees and Jesus concentrates on their partial blindness. The pronouncements regarding the door and the shepherd are part of a complicated metaphorical discourse. The pronouncement on the resurrection and the life is part of a dialogue with Martha and is followed by the raising of Lazarus. The pronouncement of "the way, the truth, and the life" falls in the Farewell Discourse. The "true vine" occurs, among other metaphors, as a part of a near allegory. Thus, none stands alone, but each is part of a rich context that aids us in understanding its meaning.[16]

The Position of Schweizer and Bultmann

It is impossible for the second parts of the formulations to be literal, unless one follows the course laid by Schweizer and Bultmann, who consider the terms symbolic titles. Even if this is done, it must rest upon the completed metaphorical process. The symbol gains its meaning from the change of meaning developed in the metaphor. For example, if one allows that Jesus is literally the light of the world, this terminology must depend on earlier usage by false messiahs and foreign deities. In these areas, the "light" metaphor must have been used to such an extent that Jesus can now contrast himself with them. By the use of the definite article, Jesus would then show himself as the only true messiah, in contrast to these others who are false.

15. Brown, *Gospel According to John (i–xii)*, 537.
16. Cerfaux, "Le Thème Littéraire Parabolique," 17.

We are not alone, however, in our rejection of these terms as symbolic titles. Juelicher stated his conviction quite clearly.[17] From the literary field, we might add the comment of Brown: "When Christ said, 'I am the light of the word,' 'I am the door and the sheepfold.' He spoke in metaphor; yet he uttered truth, not vague, nor merely approximate truth but truth of mathematical exactitude."[18] While it may seem to some that Schweizer's concept is forceful, we believe that it weakens the concepts and limits their scope.[19]

The basis for Schweizer's position can be clearly ascertained from his History of Religions research; in the Mandaean writings, the concepts used in the Gospel of John are found, not as figures of speech, but as real forms with which the deity identified himself.[20] As he proceeds to determine what literary category might fit the "I am" passages in John, he includes the metaphor and simile, together considering the two forms so much alike that he may ask if the sentence is a comparison that is poorly formed or abbreviated.[21] After eliminating the metaphor from consideration because it has a "masked" character, which cannot be considered ἀληθινὸς, he proceeds to present the terms with literal meanings. He seems to feel that figurative meanings involve weakness and inexactitude.[22] He further shows his limited definition of metaphor by insisting upon this "masked" nature of the metaphor, which causes a metaphor to cease to exist when it is understood. Such an assumption is false, for it rules out the very nature by which metaphor conveys meaning. This limited definition shows itself when he argues that the "I am" passages cannot be metaphors because they have more than one point of comparison.[23] Such is nearly always the case when we deal with metaphors.

Thus, Schweizer concludes that these pronouncements are not figurative (*uneigentlich*) metaphors but literal (*eigentlich*). Jesus is that which the expressions claim.[24]

Bultmann takes much the same position in his commentary. He concludes that Jesus begins this revelations speech with ἐγώ εἰμι language,

17. Jülicher, *Die Gleichnisse Jesu*, 56n1.
18. Brown, *World of Imagery*, 226.
19. Schulz, *Komposition*, 86; Feuillet, "Les ἐγώ εἰμι Christologiques," 213–40.
20. Schweizer, *Ego Eimi*, 82.
21. Schweizer, *Ego Eimi*, 115.
22. Schweizer, *Ego Eimi*, 117–18.
23. Schweizer, *Ego Eimi*, 120.
24. Schweizer, *Ego Eimi*, 122.

making clear statements about whom he is. This first sentence cannot be παροιμία. It cannot say, "I am like a good shepherd."[25] To arrive at this position, he presupposes such a semantic development of meaning that must take place when a metaphor is used. He finds in Hebrews 13:20 and 1 Peter 5:4 the metaphorical change of meaning that provides the basis for the title.[26] Such a presupposition eliminates any possibility of a historical basis for the speeches of Jesus and makes the speeches of Jesus that are found in John total constructions of the author. We cannot help but question whether Hebrews 13:20 and 1 Peter 5:4 could not more easily have been the product of the tradition behind John.

The Weakness of This Position

We should now like to proceed to show why we believe that the concept of the metaphor explains the intention of the author more clearly than merely considering the second segments of the "I am" proclamations of literal titles.

The Revelatory Emphasis Is Better Explained by the Metaphor

The metaphorical concept most adequately explains the revelatory implication of ἐγώ εἰμι with a predicate. It is true that there are cases where these words standing alone seem to carry a divine connotation,[27] and these terms may also carry such a connotation in certain Old Testament passages where "I am" is used with a predicate. However, two facts argue strongly against such a divine application in the Gospel of John. First, the ἐγώ εἰμι formula is not always present in the expressions of the terminology. In 9:5, the expression calling our attention to the light of the world does not have the ἐγώ. Thus, Jesus can reveal the same thought without the divine formula, ἐγώ εἰμι. In 9:9, the ἐγώ εἰμι formula stands alone. It does not have divine connotations, but rather states in simple terms the affirmation of the blind man. While Feuillet and Schweizer lay their emphasis upon the divine character of these sayings, Borgen emphasizes that they need not have this character, and brings citations from Jewish literature to support his case.[28]

---

25. Bultmann, *Das Evangelium*, 276.

26. Bultmann, *Das Evangelium*, 278.

27. Feuillet, "Les ἐγώ εἰμι Christologiques," 235; Schweizer, *Ego Eimi*, 24.

28. Borgen, *Bread from Heaven*, 59–98; see especially 72.

The "I am" passages in John carry divine implications because Jesus is divine. Thus, when Jesus says ἐγώ εἰμι, or simply εἰμι, this divine element is present because Jesus is involved.

Second, when one considers the thought of the passages, it becomes obvious that a union of terminology has taken place. The "I am" statements are thus crystallizing points of revelatory speeches containing structural elements of self-revelation.[29] If the revelation is contained in the title, we should expect the background of the title to supply the "complete background," but it does not. All attempts to provide a complete background that does not take into account the discourses or the miracles are deficient in their explanation.[30]

To come to a clear understanding of the concepts, one must come to grips with the context and the elements provided by both terms of the "revelatory formulas." The "I" provides meaning, as well as the figurative element, according to Brown.

> The stress in all of these "I am" statements is not exclusively on the "I," for Jesus also wishes to give emphasis to the predicate that tells something of his role. The predicate is not an essential definition or description of Jesus in himself; it is more a description of what he is in relation to man . . . Thus, these predicates are not static titles of autodoxology but a revelation of the divine commitment involved in the Father's sending of the Son.[31]

This implies a metaphorical process, with a change of meaning coming from a union of terms in a given context designed to form a new concept. As a result of this union, the entire metaphor may be applied to the figurative element so that it becomes a title.[32] However, this is a process that takes time, and it cannot come about on a momentary basis.

The context then becomes a preparation for the understanding of the revelation, which comes through the pronunciation. Such a context is necessary. "In the hearer's case the essential thing is preparation; we must understand from the context something of what is in the speaker's mind."[33]

29. Schnackenburg, *Das Johannesevangelium*, 137.

30. Hoskyns, *Fourth Gospel*, 367.

31. Brown, *Gospel According to John (i–xii)*, 534–35.

32. Stephen J. Brown describes this process in detail with emphasis upon the time that is necessary before the figurative element of the metaphor can assume the meaning of the entire metaphor and thus become a title. See *World of Imagery*, 40.

33. Stanford, *Greek Metaphor*, 88.

It provides the basis in the hearer's (or reader's) mind for the understanding of the new union of terms involved.

In each case, then, two basic elements are involved. That which we might call the known, the concept, or role; this might be the good shepherd, the door, the bread, etc. Then there is a second, an unknown or revealed element, which is the Christ. These two elements are united in such a way in John that they form a distinctive metaphor.

The context in which this union takes place becomes very important, for it emphasizes the segments of each element that become a part of the new union. Thus, in John, the "I am" metaphors are developed in contexts that explain the role of the figure as it relates to the Christ. These figures are often placed in contrast to other figures in order that they may bring certain important features more clearly to the minds of the hearers. Thus, we see Jesus present his metaphorical role as the bread of life, in contrast with the manna from the Exodus era. He demonstrates his role as the light of the world by healing the blind man, and then contrasts it with the partial blindness of the Pharisees (9:39–41). The role of the resurrection and the life is demonstrated by the resurrection of Lazarus, as Jesus contrasts himself as the way apart from all other ways that do not lead to God. In each case, the author intends the contrasts and the contextual background to bring out the full meaning of the metaphor.

The Definite Article Is Common in New Testament Metaphor

The second area where we find the metaphor to be a more adequate definition of the Johannine "I am" passages involves the use of the definite article in connection with the figurative element. Schweizer holds this to be one of the distinctive elements in his case for the symbolic title.[34] Our comparison of these segments of metaphors with other metaphoric uses in the New Testament has shown this use of the article to be a common part of the construction. It is deceiving for us who use German or English because the definite article would not be used in our languages. C. H. Dodd thus notes usages of the definite article common to the synoptic parable. After listing numerous examples, he says, "In such cases an English speaker would naturally use the indefinite article. Thus, our present passage should

---

34. Schweizer, *Ego Eimi*, 119–20.

be translated, 'A slave is not a permanent member of the household: a son is a permanent member.'"[35]

In addition, we have noted other cases where an analogous metaphor was used expressly. In each case, the definite article is there or implied: τὸ ἅλας τῆς γῆς (Matt 5:13); τὸ φῶς τοῦ κόσμου (Matt 5:14); ὁ λύχνος (John 5:35). In John 8:34, δοῦλος is made definite by the article before the participle, and the definite article is carried through the extension of the metaphor John presents (v. 35). In Matthew 15:14, we do not find the metaphor with the definite article, but here the article is absent because the metaphor ("blind guides") is plural. In John 10:8, the metaphor is also plural ("thieves and robbers") and comes without the definite article.

This use of the article is very close to the generic use,[36] and this usage is what one would expect when dealing with a metaphor for general classes or concepts, and not with individuals. Therefore, it is deceiving to infer from this use of the definite article that Jesus was setting himself up as the true figure against other false figures.[37] There are cases where the metaphors do contrast with false or imperfect images, but such contrast cannot be drawn from the definite article.

Other Metaphors in John

These metaphors are a part of a pattern of usage found not only here in John, but also in Matthew. It is a pattern of usage whereby the metaphor is stated or implied, and then it is followed by an extension either in a short parabolic form, a sign, or a discourse. The metaphors involve the relationship or role of a general figure in each case, and the extension reveals how elements of the figure convey associated meanings of the metaphor.

John 8:34–36

In John 8:34–36, we see an illustration of the Johannine pattern: a metaphor with a parabolic form following it, which thereby extends the meaning. The metaphor comes in verse 34: "I tell you the truth, everyone who sins is a slave to sin." The elements include "Everyone who sins," which is the literal

---

35. Dodd, *Historical Tradition*, 380, 381n1.

36. Blass et al., *Greek Grammar*, §252.

37. Schweizer, *Ego Eimi*, 123–24.

element, and "a slave to sin," which is the figurative element. The two elements are combined with the verb "is."

The importance of the metaphor comes when we consider the "parabolic form" that follows in verse 35: "Now a slave has no permanent place in the family, but a son belongs to it forever." Here we have the insecurity of the role of the servant emphasized by its contrast with the son. While the mention of Abraham (v. 33) or the Pauline development of the association (Gal 4:21–31) would call our attention to the similarity of the figures to the story of Ishmael, there is no necessity for such an allusion to be made. The figures need do no more than apply to the general situation of a servant.[38] Godet would apply an allegorical interpretation to this passage.[39] The relation between metaphor and allegory is close, and we may certainly see in verse 36 an allusion to the Christ. However, we need not go as far as describing the householder as the Father; such an application is not necessary. The point of the metaphor (i.e., the insecurity of the servant) is the main point of the passage.

John 5:35

The same phenomenon appears in John 5:35. Here again there is an explicit statement of the metaphor.[40] "John was a lamp that burned and gave light, and you chose for a time to enjoy his light." The literal element, "John," refers to John the Baptist. The figurative element is "a lamp that burned and gave light."[41] This is a metaphor that may be seen to apply to Elijah[42] or David,[43] but as C. K. Barrett rightly notes, "Lamp is a natural enough metaphor for any distinguished person and appears, e.g., in the rabbinic literature."[44] Then, the metaphor is extended to emphasize the relation of the Jews to the lamp sent from God to bear witness to them.[45] This extension (and you chose for a time to enjoy his light) does take the form of a parabolic story noted in 8:34–36, as there is no near allegorical associa-

38. Bernard, *Critical and Exegetical Commentary*, 307.

39. Godet, *Kommentar*, 339–40.

40. Hoskyns, *Fourth Gospel*, 272.

41. Strathmann, *Das Evangelium*, 104.

42. Strathmann, *Das Evangelium*, 104.

43. Bernard, *Critical and Exegetical Commentary*, 249.

44. Barrett, *Gospel*, 220.

45. Barrett, *Gospel*, 220.

tion implied. Yet the language of the metaphor unmistakably carries into the clause that follows it, so we cannot miss the extension of meaning the author intended.

John 3:29

This same phenomenon can also be used by the author of the Gospel of John without the express statement of the metaphor. In these cases, the metaphor is so strong that we cannot miss its application to the parabolic form. We might turn to the witness of John the Baptist in 3:29 to illustrate this metaphorical use. "The bride belongs to the bridegroom. The friend who attends the bridegroom waits and listens for him, and is full of joy when he hears the bridegroom's voice." The context makes it clear that the Baptist is saying, "I am the friend of the bridegroom." Thus, John's joy is complete.[46] We are left to infer that the Christ is the bridegroom, and possibly that the bride is the church.[47] Thus, we would come once more to the position where an allegorical interpretation is possible but not necessary.

The parabolic form does not need a special story, but refers to a general description of a Judean wedding.[48] The role of the characters is normal. In our context, the role of the friend of the bridegroom determines all, for it answers the question the Baptist wishes to answer: "What is my relation to Jesus?" The other roles—i.e., the bridegroom and the bride—must be seen in relation to it. We cannot help but say "Jesus is the bridegroom," but this metaphor takes meaning only from the position of the Baptist.

John 5:19–20

The same phenomenon is possibly at work in 5:19–20, although here if there is a metaphor, it is so strong it nearly disappears. Jesus appears to be putting forth the normal relation of a father and son. The father desires to set an example for the son. However, the Johannine emphasis on Jesus as the Son of God is so strong that we wonder if the author intended the metaphorical background. Note especially verse 18, where the equation between God and the Father is expressly stated.

46. Bultmann, *Das Evangelium*, 127.
47. Barrett, *Gospel*, 186.
48. Strathmann, *Das Evangelium*, 78.

Nonetheless, we cannot deny that the relationship between the father and son is built on the natural relationship found in Hebrew thought.

> Here too the Evangelist builds upon the human analogy of the rela-
> tion between father and son, for he substitutes the normal human
> verb to love (ἀγαπάω) for the rarer verb he had used in the parallel
> passage in 3:35 . . . The understanding of the opening verses of the
> discourse depends upon the recognition that the function of a son
> is to reproduce the thought and action of his father. This is indeed
> the fundamental doctrine of the relation between father and son
> in Hebrew biblical thought.[49]

We might note this natural relationship, especially in verse 20, where the usual Johannine word for love (ἀγαπάω) is exchanged for a word (φιλέω) that more expressive of the parental relationship. C. H. Dodd goes even further to show that the relationship between father and son also colored the terminology so that a master craftsman was called "father" and his apprentice "son." Therefore, this parabolic form in John is not simply a creation of the author for the purpose of his theology; it builds upon contextual understandings of the day.[50]

This similarity to the natural world in fact pervades all of the Johannine metaphoric uses. These expressions, which in some cases might be called parabolic, are extended metaphors built chiefly on one role, or relationships that result from that role. As in the case here, the saying is understandable without the metaphorical application,[51] but it does not take on its full meaning until the metaphorical meaning is also expressed.

SIMILARITIES BETWEEN METAPHORS
IN JOHN AND MATTHEW

C. H. Dodd's note that this parabolic form is very similar in form to Matthew 5:15 and Luke 8:16 causes us to turn to these passages, as they reflect synoptic parallels to the metaphors we find in John.[52]

---

49. Hoskyns, *Fourth Gospel*, 268.

50. Dodd, "Une Parabole," 111.

51. Dodd, "Une Parabole," 108.

52. Dodd, "Une Parabole," 115; Brown, *Gospel According to John (i–xii)*, 218.

Matthew 5:14–15

This saying begins with a metaphor, "ὑμεῖς ἐστε τὸ φῶς τοῦ κόσμου," so that the metaphor of "the light of the world" then controls the thought of the parabolic form that follows. Lohmeyer notes that the author uses three different words for light, each varying with the part of the pericope in which it stands.[53] This is in Johannine character.[54] The saying assumes the following pattern: a) metaphor (Matt 5:14a); b) the first extension (v. 14b); and c) the second extension (v. 15). In the Lucan parallel (Luke 8:16), not only is the metaphor dropped, but the first extension of meaning is different, and the context and application are strikingly different from Matthew. In Matthew, the metaphor is applied to exemplary discipleship. In Luke, it is used as an illustration of our moral situation. Matthew thus follows the Johannine pattern much more closely.

Matthew 5:13

Matthew 5:13 reflects the same basic structure: a metaphor with a literary form appended to extend the meaning of the metaphor. "You are the salt of the earth. But if the salt loses its saltiness, how can it be made salty again?" The parabolic form is bound with a conditional sentence revolving around the taste of salt. In Mark 9:50 and Luke 14:34–35, we have basically the same parabolic form, but without the metaphor introducing it. In both of these latter cases, the figure maintains its literal form. It is introduced with a literal expression, "Salt is good." Matthew follows the pattern of the Johannine metaphor, while Mark and Luke do not.

Matthew 15:14

In Matthew 15:14 we have another very striking metaphorical expression with a parabolic form added to extend its context to the hearers: "Leave them; they are blind guides. If a blind man leads a blind man, both will fall into a pit." Again, the extension here takes the form of a conditional sentence, and we find the same parabolic form Matthew uses to extend the meaning in Luke. In Luke 6:39, it appears without the metaphor or the Matthean context that brought it forth. In this case in Luke, the form is

53. Lohmeyer, *Das Evangelium des Matthäus*, 100.
54. Freed, "Variations," 167–97.

called a "παραβολή," although it probably refers to the saying as no more than a proverb. In each of these metaphorical sayings, we have found in Matthew the parabolic form connected with it. The saying also appears in Mark or Luke, but without the metaphor. Therefore, in the Synoptic Gospels, metaphors at times fulfill very different functions.

The similarity between the Johannine metaphor and those metaphorical sayings in Matthew is thus close but not exact. In each case, the extension of meaning connected with the context of the metaphor is not a special case, but something very general, something we would find in everyday functions of the role.

THE METAPHORICAL DISCOURSES

A look at the Old Testament background of the word "παροιμία" is fitting at this point. This word is used by John to describe the metaphorical discourse in chapter 10. In the Greek, we have distinctive classifications and various words for the classifications of the various figures of speech. In the Hebrew, one word, *maschal*, describes all. Brown, Driver, and Briggs show that this word is applied to: 1) a proverbial saying; 2) a byword; 3) a prophetic figure; 4) a similitude or parable; 5) a poem; and 6) a saying of ethical wisdom.[55] This breadth of meaning is further echoed by Jülicher, when he illumines the general nature of the term. He shows that *maschal* may be used of long or short passages with or without the usual particle of comparison, or even as an allegory.[56] There is a strong connection between the word and the prophetic office (Num 23:7, 18; 24:3, 15, 20–21, 23; Isa 14:4; Mic 2:4; Hab 2:6—the latter three being proverbs that the prophets used to warn about the future). Thus, there may also be an element of revelation in the New Testament parable, as the parables of Jesus sometimes fill a role similar to that of the Jewish prophets.[57]

In the LXX, the word is a synonym for παραβολή. Παροιμία gains more usage in the later periods. *Maschal* appears in Proverbs 1:1, where the LXX translates it as παροιμία, while Aquila uses παραβολή. In 3 Kings 5:12 (1 Kings 4:12 in the English Bible), the thousand sayings of Solomon are παραβολή in the LXX. In Sirach 47:17, both παροιμία and παραβολή are

---

55. Brown et al., *Hebrew and English Lexicon*, 604–5.

56. Jülicher, *Die Gleichnisse Jesu*, 37.

57. Cerfaux, "Le Thème Littéraire Parabolique," 15.

attributed to him; thus, the two words may be treated as synonyms.[58] Both share in the background of the Hebrew *maschal*, which does not limit them to what we consider the synoptic parable. The use of παραβολή refers to a mere proverb, so παραβολή and parable cannot necessarily be equated.

Such is the Hebrew background of παροιμία as it comes into the New Testament, where it is used three times in John and once in 2 Peter 2:22. In John, the word is used in relation to the story of the shepherd and the door (10:1–5) and also in 16:25 and 29, where it is contrasted with παρρησία. There the term refers to a "dark saying" or "riddle" in need of interpretation.[59] When we turn to John 10, there are very few rules that can be applied to explain the interpretation given. Torm is correct when he says that the mixed forms of allegory and parabolic speech are frequently associated in rabbinic writings,[60] so we can classify the material and the figures of speech, but we cannot "create absolute norms to which the concrete material can always be made to conform."[61]

We shall now turn to the metaphorical discourses in John to observe what happens. The metaphor is important in each case, but we are bound to rely upon the overall context. This involves considering the background of the Old Testament and other elements within the narrative necessary for interpretation. Expansions within the narratives draw in elements of the background applicable to the metaphor,[62] and four discourses we shall consider in John include: 6:27–58; 4:8–15; 10:1–16; and 15:1–7. Each possesses its own characteristics, and each shows the author's distinctive approaches to the metaphor employed.

The Bread of Life (6:27–58)

The discourse on the bread of life is built upon an especially elaborate use of metaphor. The metaphors of the passage are used without the assistance of any parabolic forms, and the passages involve only the development of the metaphors.

---

58. Hatch, *Essays in Biblical Greek*, 67.

59. Hauck, "παροιμία," 854; cf. also Stanford, *Greek Metaphor*, 23.

60. Torm, *Hermeneutik des Neuen Testaments*, 115–16.

61. Dahl, "Parables of Growth," 136.

62. Cerfaux, "Le Thème Littéraire Parabolique," 21.

The Basic Elements of the Metaphor

As with most Johannine metaphors, the development comes on the basis of contrast. Such a contrast is expressed early in the discourse (vv. 27–31), where the living bread is contrasted with the manna of the Exodus. The life-giving element of the new heavenly bread becomes an important feature of the new bread. We have this aspect stated positively in verse 33 (ζωὴν διδοὺς); verses 35 and 48 (ὁ ἄρτος τῆς ζωῆς); verses 39, 44, and 54 (ἀναστήσω αὐτὸ ἐν τῇ ἐσχάτῃ ἡμέρᾳ; see also verse 40 for an expanded form); verses 51 and 58 (ζήσει εἰς τὸν αἰῶνα); verse 54 (ἔχει ζωὴν αἰώνιον); verse 57 (ζήσει δι' ἐμέ); and negatively in verses 39, 50, 53, and 58.

The contrast is further emphasized by the use of ἀληθινόν in verse 32 and ἀληθής in verse 55. Such is the method by which John draws out the new meaning through his use of metaphors. These words related to truth are used in relation to the vine in 15:1, and with relation to the light in 1:9. The way and the door are not expressed in relation to concepts of truth, but by negative additions that eliminate the other ways, and the other doors as invalid (10:8; 14:6). The good shepherd is not contrasted with other shepherds, but with the hirelings. Only the phrase "the resurrection and the life" (11:25) is not explicitly contrasted. This latter passage shows that we cannot infer such a contrast from the use of the definite article.[63] Such an inference would require Jesus to be set in contrast to all other resurrections and all other lives as the true life. We cannot support such from the text.

The background of the bread metaphor lies chiefly in the Old Testament. Borgen rightly emphasizes the use of verse 31 as the basis upon which Jesus proceeds to build the rest of the discourse.[64] Strathmann shows that the Jewish demand for a sign does not come from the fact that they have not recognized the feeding of the five thousand on the previous day as a sign, but that they wished a daily feeding that would imitate the Exodus wonder.[65]

In verse 32, Jesus takes this passage, which the Jews have quoted, and changes it in accord with rabbinic midrashic practice so that it applies to himself: "it is not Moses . . . but it is my Father who gives you the true bread"; "By these changes, Jesus indicates that the Old Testament is being fulfilled now in his work. The manna given by Moses was not the real bread

---

63. See pages pp.98–99.
64. Borgen, *Bread from Heaven*, 59–98.
65. Strathmann, *Das Evangelium*, 115–16.

from heaven which the Old Testament speaks of. It is Jesus' teaching."[66] We see Jesus return to the background again in what must be considered the climactic part of the discourse (v. 49). The contrast between the new bread and the manna of the Exodus forms the basis of the development of the metaphor.

The Old Testament Background Is Expanded with New Christian Elements

In the positive development of the metaphor, Jesus naturally goes beyond the Old Testament background. As Barrett points out,

> The notion of heavenly bread is rooted in the Old Testament and Jewish thought, and arises out of the gift of the manna. It is not however purely Jewish; "the idea of heavenly food, which nourishes unending life, with the Greeks goes back as far as Homer and is equally at home in the East" (Bauer, 100, with many references). The background material is completed, in the threefold manner characteristic of John (Jewish, pagan and Christian), by the occurrence of bread in both the miraculous and parabolic elements of the synoptic tradition, and in the eucharist.[67]

The change of meaning in the metaphor requires all of these elements. Thus, we find certain Christian elements also present. One cannot introduce the "I," or the Jesus element, into the metaphor without transforming the meaning. Thus, the elements of eternal life and of the Eucharist become important throughout the passage,[68] and Christian elements are evident within the development.

The author develops the meaning by mixing metaphors so that he can draw a thoroughly Christian application. Thus, "he who believes in me will never be thirsty" (v. 35b) is added to the metaphor of the bread in the discourse, and we might consider this a repetition of the water-of-life metaphor in John 4 if it were not for verses 53 and 56: "whoever eats my flesh and drinks my blood." This addition directs our thoughts to the Lord's

---

66. Brown, *Gospel According to John (i–xii)*, 262.

67. Barrett, *Gospel*, 243; cf. Brown, *Gospel According to John (i–xii)*, 266; and Dodd, *Interpretation*, 335.

68. Borgen, *Bread from Heaven*, 78.

Supper,[69] and such mixing of the metaphors shows the emergence of Christian influence on the proper development of the meaning of the metaphor.

The Seven Statements of the Metaphor

Another distinction of the Bread of Life discourse is the number of times (seven) the metaphor is stated, and each restatement, with the exception of verses 35 and 48, is different. The first statement of the metaphor (v. 33) introduces the basic elements of the metaphor as it is developed in the discourse: "For the bread of God is he who comes down from heaven and gives life to the world." These elements, descending from heaven and giving life, make up the distinctive elements we find in the metaphor developed elsewhere in the chapter. Scholars are divided on whether this metaphor should be interpreted personally, as it would relate to Jesus, or impersonally, as it would relate to the bread.

Raymond E. Brown is probably right in stating that the ambiguity probably shows that the author intended both.[70] Not only is the impersonal character understood by the people involved (v. 34), but the words of Jesus also state the metaphor impersonally twice (vv. 50, 58), where the subject of the metaphor is not ἐγώ εἰμι but οὗτός ἐστιν. On the other hand, there are four times when the metaphor is stated personally (vv. 35, 41, 48, 51).

None of these seven statements is an exact repetition of the metaphor, with the exception of verses 35 and 48, but all are built around the two elements we have noted in verse 33. The first time the metaphor is applied to Jesus (v. 35), we deal only with the element, "I am the bread of life." The second statement comes in the miscomprehending question of the crowd, and it omits the concept of life in favor of the heavenly origin, "I am the bread that came down from heaven" (v. 41). The restatement in verse 48 duplicates verse 35, and it is not until we find the impersonal statement in verse 50 that both elements are drawn together for the second time: "But here is the bread that comes down from heaven, which a man may eat and not die." Here the impersonal metaphor is stated in terms of the heavenly origin, with the life-giving element stated negatively in the result clause that follows the metaphor.

In verse 51a, we have the second and last complete statement of the metaphor, "I am the living bread that came down from heaven," which

69. Strathmann, *Das Evangelium*, 116.

70. Brown, *Gospel According to John (i–xii)*, 232–33.

differs from verse 33 in its personal nature, and in that it is more concise. Also, the usual form, "ὁ ἄρτος τῆς ζωῆς," is exchanged for "ὁ ἄρτος ὁ ζῶν," as this statement is the climax of the passage. The remainder of the discourse has a distinct Eucharistic tone on the basis of verse 51b. Thus, we turn from the development of the metaphor to its application; i.e., the thought does not continue with the aspects of the heavenly, life-giving bread, but the "eating" of it as a means of appropriating its benefit. Only in verse 58 does the metaphor reappear. Here it is stated impersonally, as it is in verse 50, but the participle related to the bread is aorist and not present, where the life-giving element is stated positively.

The varying statements of the metaphor create a strong argument against considering the metaphors as titles or symbols, and the changes of meaning found in the various metaphorical expressions of the chapter are only possible when one considers them as metaphors. The use of a figurative expression as a symbolic title requires a fixed form for the figure, and we do not find this in the Bread of Life discourse.

The Movement between the Literal and the Figurative

The final element in this chapter that is important for our study of the metaphor involves the ability of the author to move back and forth between the literal and the figurative. We have already noted the form basis which the figure "bread of life" finds in the Old Testament, and all of these references to the Old Testament are literal expressions. In addition to these passages (vv. 31–34, 49), we should pay close attention to verses 36–40. In verse 33, the heavenly element is stated in literal terms. This statement becomes the basis for the first figurative expression of the heavenly origin: "For the bread of God is he who comes down from heaven and gives life to the world." The statement of the metaphor by the Jews can only come from a combination of the thought in verse 35, "I am the bread of life" (figurative), and in verse 38, "I have come down from heaven" (literal). Thus, the Jews speak (verse 41) correctly, combining both statements. Unless we accept Bultmann's reconstruction of the passage, which places verse 51a before either, this is the only explanation we can make with regard to the murmur of the people.[71]

In verses 42–47, we continue in the literal meaning once more. Yet even in this section, we find both of the emphasized aspects of the metaphor predominant. The irony of the question regarding the parents of Jesus

71. Bultmann, *Das Evangelium*, 163.

points us to the bread's heavenly origin.[72] The ability of the Christ to give life is connected with the resurrection (v. 44), and because it is received as a result of faith, both themes are developed literally. Only in verse 48 do we return to the metaphorical use, although in verse 49 we are again literal with the reference to the Exodus account of the giving of the manna. Verses 50–51 are again figurative, as is the remainder of the passage, being built on the application of the metaphor for the believing benefit of the reader.

The Water of Life (4:8–15)

While the water-of-life theme is closely related to the bread-of-life theme, they separated by chapter 5, which features the first set of debates between Jesus and Jewish leaders in Jerusalem. Following John 6, the living water theme is also picked up in John 7:37–39, so the interplay between these metaphors is palpable.

The Similarities with Chapter 6

This metaphorical discourse stands in contrast to the discourse of the bread of life. Both passages are similar, as the general context in each case is based on parallel elements. Jesus' request for a drink calls attention to the role of water, just as the feeding of the five thousand did for bread. The Old Testament basis of both figures is clear, as water from the well is associated with the patriarch Jacob, and the bread of life is related to the manna Moses gave. Further, in each situation, the element of the believer's insight for the proper interpretation is necessary. In John 6, the discourse builds the picture of the bread of life in such a way that one cannot miss the Eucharistic element, and in John 4, the irony of verses 12–14 hinges upon the Johannine view of what Jesus offers (7:37–39) for the full understanding to be discerned.[73]

In addition, we might note similarities of contrasts regarding the objects involved. As noted above, the double meaning of τὸ ὕδωρ τὸ ζῶν means both "living water" and "running water."[74] This dual meaning provides the basis for the contrast, as the living earthly water (running water) is juxtaposed against with the true, heavenly, life-giving water. The woman's

72. Bultmann, *Das Evangelium*, 59–63.

73. Bultmann, *Das Evangelium*, 63–64.

74. Bultmann, *Das Evangelium*, 37.

miscomprehension is exposed in her inability to lift her perspective above the material (v. 15).

A further striking similarity between these scenarios involves the life-producing features of bread and water, as living water (τὸ ὕδωρ τὸ ζῶν; 4:10–11) leads to life (εἰς τὸν αἰῶνα; 4:14; 6:51, 58), just as bread did (εἰς ζωὴν αἰώνιον; 4:14; 6:47). The parallelism between the most expressive statements of chapters 4 and 6 is also striking: "If a man eats of this bread, he will live forever. This bread is my flesh, which I will give for the life of the world" (6:51b); and, "Everyone who drinks this water will be thirsty again, but whoever drinks the water I give him will never thirst" (4:14). Both emphasize the giving work of Jesus (δίδωμι), and in both cases a nearly identical request evokes the figurative expansion of Jesus (6:34; 4:15).

The Search for the Metaphorical Statement

In spite of all these similarities, we are faced with one surprising difference. In John 6, the "I am" reference is expressed seven times; in John 4, not at all. This has led commentators to debate the difference between the simple use of a metaphor and its use within an "I am" statement. Bultmann is among those who suggest that the living water refers to the revelation of Christ;[75] Bernard and others suggest that it refers to the Holy Spirit.[76] We believe Strathmann has correctly noted the weakness of this position,[77] although Brown and others feel that both suggestions could well be applied.[78]

We propose a fourth alternative, given that the discourse is based upon the unexpressed metaphor, "ἐγώ εἰμι τὸ ὕδωρ τὸ ζῶν."[79] The similarities between chapters 4 and 6 would lead us in this direction, even though it is not rendered explicitly in the text. The concept of "giving" the water of life is also important, as Jesus "is" that which he gives.[80] Just as Jesus gave light to the blind man, he also said, "I am the light of the world." He raised Lazarus and said, "I am the resurrection and the life." He fed the five thousand and said, "I am the bread of life." Why then should we feel the need to separate the water of life from the person of Jesus? Such a separation is especially

75. Bultmann, *Das Evangelium*, 136.

76. Bernard, *Critical and Exegetical Commentary*, 138.

77. Strathmann, *Das Evangelium*, 85.

78. Brown, *Gospel According to John (i–xii)*, 178–79.

79. Against Brown, *Gospel According to John (i–xii)*, 179.

80. Brown, *Gospel According to John (i–xii)*, 20.

difficult when we find that the goal of the conversation with the woman is none other than faith in Jesus as Messiah, ἐγώ εἰμι, ὁ λαλῶν σοι (v. 26).

The Door and the Good Shepherd (10:1–18)

The metaphors developed in John 10 pose a different set of challenges, as Jesus claims to be both the shepherd of the sheep and the door of the sheepfold. Is this mixing of metaphors a clumsy accident, or is some form of development at work in the design of the author? A closer look at the contexts will be instructive.

The Similarities with the Preceding Discourses

The metaphorical discourse in John 10:1–18 follows some of the same characteristics noted in the two earlier discourses. The Old Testament forms the background for the figures mentioned,[81] but as in previous cases, the biblical background is not in itself sufficient. (The metaphor demands that new elements come into the meaning.) Thus, we note the strong emphasis in the second portion of the discourse on laying down the life (vv. 11, 17–18). With Barrett, "This feature (lay down life) of the parable is not derived from the Old Testament or any other source nor does it enter into the synoptic shepherd parables; it is based specifically upon the crucifixion as a known historical event."[82] In verse 16, we see the shepherd declaring that he will draw in sheep from other folds, which can only be understood as a reference to the diversity and unity of the church.[83]

The author also retains his ability to move between the figurative and the literal. In verse 9, we should expect τί to refer to the sheep (τὸ πρόβατον), yet we have the masculine τίς, which points us away from the figure to the literal person.[84] The narrator also leaves this figure of speech in verses 17–18, where Jesus speaks of the Father in an obvious reference to the impending crucifixion.

For the most part, the similarity ends here, as the discourse has a unique structure. The first five verses are described in the sixth verse as a

81. Barrett, "Old Testament," 163; cf. also Barrett, *Gospel*, 305, 308; Hoskyns, *Fourth Gospel*, 387.

82. Barrett, *Gospel*, 311.

83. Kiefer, *Die Hirtenrede*, 73.

84. Kiefer, *Die Hirtenrede*, 17.

παροιμία. The next verses (vv. 7–10) revolve around the figure of the door with two ἐγώ εἰμι statements, whereas the figure of the good shepherd becomes predominant in verses 11–18, with two more ἐγώ εἰμι statements.

The Παροιμία of Verses 1–5

In the first five verses, we have a figurative presentation revolving around the figures of thieves, robbers, the door, and the shepherd and the sheep. In the first two verses, the shepherd and the thief and robber are contrasted in their relation to the door. In the remaining three verses, the normal role of the Palestinian shepherd is expounded, yet we have very little indication as to the explanatory contents of verses 7–18.

Attempts to divide the section into two original parables fail on three counts.[85] First, the division between 3a and 3b is forced, because the two sections are so intricately bound together. The words "θύρα" and "ποιμήν" appear adjacent to one another in verse two. The word "ποιμήν" never appears in the second part of the pericope, but it is only the antecedent of pronouns and the understood subject of verbs. While we may say that verses 1–3a deal largely with the door, we must say that verses 2–5 deal with the shepherd.

Second, such a division does not clarify the "explanation" that follows it. In verses 1–2, the thieves and robbers are contrasted with the shepherd as both relate to the door. In verses 7–10, the thieves and robbers are contrasted with the door. The shepherd is contrasted with the hireling in verses 11–13. It is true that 14b relates to 3b and 4b-5. But so does 8b, "the sheep did not listen to them." The element in 4a relates most clearly to verse 9 (again to the section of the door). Thus, there is no clear-cut division within the παροιμία as to what relates to the door and what relates to the shepherd.

Third, attempts to divide are confounded by the fact that Jesus is identified with both of the key elements. Thus, the attempts to divide the passage here find no clear basis in what follows as a combination of elements. In the metaphor, this combination of meanings with both aspects as well as the similarity of the context promotes a mixing of the images.[86] Verse 6 provides a natural break in the discourse, where John calls the saying of Jesus a παροιμία and then proceeds to say that the people did not understand what he said.

85. Robinson, "Parable," 233–40.
86. Barrett, Gospel, 306.

I Am the Door (Verses 7–10)

In verses 7–10, Jesus is the door, and in verse 7 Jesus is called ἡ θύρα τῶν προβάτων, while in verse 9 he is merely called ἡ θύρα. These "I am" passages divide the section, but they both also relate to the thieves and robbers. The contrast in application can be made because Jesus is both the door and the shepherd. This does not mean that we need to seek a union of the two functions, as some have done by attempting to show that the shepherd of the near east became the door of the fold by lying in the doorway to sleep.[87] The author maintains a separation of the metaphors in explanations, yet both metaphors in these explanations have a common element: "Jesus." We can thus expect that when they appear in the same context, we shall find some resemblance between them.

The resemblances become stronger when we recall the method of the author, who takes main features of the παροιμία in verses 1–5 and develops the meaning metaphorically. Thus, the story of verses 1–5 is not explained as a parable or a point drawn from that story, but rather, the meaning is explained on the basis of the main character and object of the discourse. The development of the subject does not reside in the meaning of the terms found in the beginning, but it rather abides in the deeper meanings of the concepts.[88] This is a total subjugation of the story to the application, and yet, the reasoning of the author moves from the application back to the story.

The metaphorical nature of the discourse again becomes apparent in verse 8. Here the thieves and robbers are identified metaphorically: "All who ever came before me were thieves and robbers." This metaphor relates to verse 1, and C. K. Barrett and Spitta are probably correct in relating this reference to false messiahs who had come earlier.[89] This second metaphor does not give the passage an allegorical nature, as the metaphors in an allegory must replace the figures in the story. The change in relationship we have noted between the παροιμία and its interpretation precludes any such replacement. The secondary figures, such as the thieves and robbers, are presented as they relate to the main figures. They may or may not be identified (note the lack of identification for the hirelings below), and yet, they find their function as they relate to the main metaphor being developed.

---

87. Bishop, "Door of the Sheep," 307–09.

88. Kiefer, *Die Hirtenrede*, 39.

89. Barrett, *Gospel*, 308; Spitta, "Die Hirtengleichnisse," 68–73.

This relationship explains the full meaning of the metaphor, and thus the function of the secondary metaphors must ever be held in supportive relation to the main metaphor.

This metaphorical development is evident when we see the contrast between the two statements. In verses 7–8, the emphasis is upon the function of the door in relation to the entrance of the thief and robber. In verses 9–10, the emphasis is upon the function of the door providing security for the sheep. In both cases, the figure of the door is bound metaphorically with Jesus, and this relation is expanded through the explication of the relationships involved in the metaphors. The other figures are secondary.

I Am the Good Shepherd (Verses 11–18)

When we turn to verses 11–18 and the metaphor dealing with the good shepherd, many of the same characteristics are present. The metaphor is stated twice, and both times it is referenced with the exact same terminology: "ὁ ποιμὴν ὁ καλὸς." This is the only time in the Gospel where a metaphor always falls in the same terminology, whereas Jesus is merely a ποιμὴν in verse 2.

This movement of the figure away from the pattern of the παροιμία (vv. 1–5) is even more striking, as none of the elements remain the same in verses 11–13. In verses 1–5, the shepherd was set in contrast to thieves and robbers (vv. 1–2) and ἀλλότριος (v. 5). In verses 11–13, the shepherd is contrasted with the hireling, but the hireling does not kill, as the thief. He merely flees in the face of danger (the coming of the wolf), caring for his own welfare and not that of the sheep.

In this passage, we have a parabolic extension of the meaning of the metaphor following the pattern we have seen in Matthew 5:13–14 and John 8:34–35. The metaphor eliminates the passage from being a true parable, and yet, if the passage were an allegory, it would require an identification of the hireling and the wolf. The pattern, however, does not lead us to seek this identification. We do not have a story that was specifically fabricated as an allegory, but here we have a general set of metaphors, relating to the roles of shepherds and hirelings.[90]

This general nature of the figures as they relate to the main metaphor is also found in the relation of the shepherd and the sheep. All that is said about the sheep is that which explicates their relation to the shepherd.

90. Westcott, *Gospel*, 154;. Müller, *Das Heilsgeschehen*, 57–58.

Although no explicit identification of the sheep is made in the discourse, the close relation of shepherd and sheep is the main thrust. Yet, as important as the role of the sheep is to our metaphor (what is a shepherd without sheep?), we find no specific demands upon the role of the sheep, overall.[91] They are totally subordinate to the function of the shepherd, and the importance of the passage revolves around the generic figures of sheep as Jesus' disciples, as they are metaphorically related to the messianic role of Jesus as the Christ.

We also see a distinct movement of thought in this passage from the presentation of metaphors toward the thematic thrust of the παροιμία in the repeated reference to "laying down the life" of the shepherd out of his love for the sheep. Such is not found in verses 1–5, but in verse 11b it becomes the basis for the extension of the metaphor dealing with the hireling. While the passage is overall figurative, however, the concept of laying down one's life is used literally in verse 15 and verses 17–18, undoubtedly referring to the crucifixion. Bultmann would allow the first to refer merely to the duty of a good shepherd to risk his life for his sheep,[92] and this interpretation is possible if we treat the figure involved as a parable or simile. As a simile, a certain separation is maintained, which would allow us to separate the action of the Christ from the role or function of the shepherd. The particle "as" keeps the two separate, so each reference remains literal. We do not have such a separation, however, when we deal with the metaphor, as the two aspects become one. The duty of the shepherd to risk his life for his sheep becomes an important aspect in the change of meaning. As the concepts become united, they are seen to refer to the coming crucifixion,[93] connecting the earlier reference with the literal references (vv. 17–18).

In spite of all of this movement away from original concepts, there is a striking dependence found within these five verses. The role of a shepherd—being known by his sheep—forms an important part of the role of the shepherd in verses 3b–5. In verse 14b, this same element becomes a part of the second "I am" expression, and serves to emphasize the interconnection between the interpretation and the παροιμία. This connection and the movement of thought from the first five verses of the chapter mark the discourse. In the first two discourses, we discussed the view that there was no παροιμία upon which the author could build metaphorically. Rather, he

91. Müller, *Das Heilsgeschehen*, 55.
92. Bultmann, *Das Evangelium*, 282n2.
93. Mueller, *Das Heilsgeschehen*, 56; Hoskyns, *Fourth Gospel*, 60–61.

was able to build upon events that were a part of the context (in chapter 6 the feeding of the five thousand, and in chapter 4 the desire for a drink of water). Here, the παροιμία forms the background, and the interpretation that follows is bound together with it by the chief roles in the παροιμία. However, new elements in the interpretation and the changes of meaning mark it as distinct in its form. These new elements prevent us from considering it a mere interpretation, as might be found with the parable of the sower in the Synoptics.

The Problem of Identification

The problem, then, of naming what we have defined becomes greater. We have avoided raising the question up to this point by avoiding the translation of the Greek παροιμία. Our earlier exploration of this term[94] shows that, while the term was usually used as a synonym for παραβολή, it should not merely be limited in its use to the synoptic parable. This is particularly striking in John, where παροιμία is used as a contrast with παρρησία (open, clear speech).

Thus, we hesitate to use the word "parable" to describe the relation of verses 1–5 to the remainder of the passage. The fact that "παροιμία," a synonym for "παραβολή," is used is not strong enough to outweigh the striking differences between the parable and what we find here. One must say, with Dahl, that the account of the good shepherd is in the form of a true parable that contains metaphorical elements;[95] or, we must go with Jeremias and allow that we have a "bad parable which involves poetic style, allegorizing and paraphrasing."[96] Both admit the need to define further the relation of verses 1–5 to the interpretation that follows, so the use of "parable" would here be confusing.[97] The movement of thought and the addition of new elements do not make for good parabolic interpretation, and the parallel structure found between verses 7–10 and verses 11–14 makes us hesitate to consider verses 11–13 a second parable.

We would also hesitate for the same reasons to consider the passage in verses 1–5 an allegory. An allegory is not just a speech made up of

94. See pages 104–105.

95. Dahl, "Gleichnis und Parabel," 1619.

96. Jeremias, "ποιμήν," 494.

97. Cerfaux, "Le Thème Littéraire Parabolique," 18; cf. Torm, *Hermeneutik des Neuen Testaments*, 115.

metaphorical elements; it involves a replacement of terms.[98] The inability to read the interpretation of the story in verses 1–5 eliminates this possibility. In addition, we are faced with the difficulty that two main figures of the story carry the same meaning; Jesus is both the door and the shepherd.[99]

This, however, leaves us with no name to describe the function we have identified, and we should feel most at home in calling the passage a "riddle" or a "dark saying."[100] These choices agree with Hauck, who chooses "dark saying," and Kiefer, who uses "riddle," to describe these metaphorical references.[101]

This terminology is chosen with the knowledge that we are involved with more than a mere comparison of terms, but rather "the notion of a mysterious saying full of compressed thought."[102] It is a saying where the meaning does not come from the story, but the meaning gives the story its significance.[103] It differs strongly from the parable that is built upon a comparison of two realities. In a parable, one reasons from the figure to the application laid alongside it,[104] whereas here we reason in the opposite fashion. The metaphors used to interpret it come in the form of what Stanford calls "developed or continued metaphor," and this is what we have chosen to call extended metaphors.

The True Vine (15:1–8)

The Old Testament Background

While the vine was originally Israel (Hos 10:1; Isa 5:3–7; Jer 2:21; Ps 79[80]:8–12), the LXX makes the connection between the vine and the Son of Man (Ps 79[80]:14–16).[105] This symbol for Israel also became a

---

98. Jülicher, *Die Gleichnisse Jesu*, 58; although Jülicher considers the passage an allegory, cf. 116; Dahl, "Parables of Growth," 137.

99. Spitta, "Die Hirtengleichnisse," 67.

100. See pages [x-ref] of this book.

101. Hauck, "παροιμία," 854; Kiefer, *Die Hirtenrede*, 81–83; Stanford, *Greek Metaphor*, 23.

102. Westcott, *Gospel*, 152.

103. Kiefer, *Die Hirtenrede*, 82, cf. also 14.

104. Stanford, *Greek Metaphor*, 24.

105. Dodd, *Interpretation*, 82.

messianic symbol in 2 Baruch, as Winter shows.[106] Again, the complete picture only comes to light when we consider the Christian implications of the metaphor. The change of meaning involved cannot be separated from the context of the Lord's Supper that had probably just been completed.[107] The event may provide a point of departure for the discourse following the pattern in the discourses dealing with the water of life and the bread of life.

Here also the author finds great freedom to move between the literal and figurative, and verses 1 and 2 form the basis of the discussion. They employ the metaphors and are largely figurative, although the striking exception, ἐγώ εἰμι in verse 2, shows the closeness of the identification. According to the figure, we understand "every branch in the vine" to be a reference to believers, and Christ is the vine. The literal "then" intrudes sharply, because in verses 3–4 ("you are already clean") the literal sense continues. The application in verse 3 comes from the metaphorical ὑμεῖς τὰ κλήματα, which is first used in verse 5. In verse 4 we have a simile, one of the few in John, and this is conveyed via literal speech, as Jülicher has shown.[108] This demonstrates the limited nature of the simile, bringing only one *tertium comparationis* before our minds, contrasted with the metaphor, which is capable of a whole set of concepts or relationships.

We return to the figurative reference in verse 5 with the second pair of metaphorical statements, yet in verse 5b, the identification of the disciples with branches is so close that we find the use of the second person plural (δύνασθε). This literal expression continues until verse 6b, when we return to the figure and the vine and branches.[109] Verse 7 is again literal, with only a reference to "bearing much fruit" in verse 8.

The "Near" Allegorical Relationship

As close as these similarities are with other discourses, we again must note striking differences between this discourse and the others. Most striking is the great increase in the allegorical character. We do not have one or two metaphorical identifications, but three that identify all of the main characters in the figurative expression. One is able to interchange the elements of the metaphor and retain the meaning. The author himself makes such

106. Winter, *On the Trial of Jesus*, 51.
107. Bernard, *Critical and Exegetical Commentary*, 478.
108. Jülicher, *Die Gleichnisse Jesu*, 188, 193.
109. Barrett, *Gospel*, 398.

interchanges in verse 2 (ἐν ἐμοὶ) and verse 5 (δύνασθε). We are not able to approach the riddle in chapter 10, however, in the same manner, although the characteristic was considered in some of the shorter metaphorical expressions (e.g. 3:29). As in that case, we do not deal with a special story created specifically to suit the allegorical purposes of the author. Rather, we have here a general statement that is true of growing vines in Palestine, whose meaning is then yoked to the author's thrust in the narrative.

"The change in form of the parabolic material appears in the fact that (a) no clear story is told; we do not hear the fate of a particular vine or vineyard but rather certain observations on viticulture and (b) that the whole symbolism is governed by the opening words ἐγώ εἰμι."[110] There is also a greater emphasis upon the secondary roles. In chapter 10, no demand was made on the role of the sheep, but here there are admonitions connected with the role of the disciples as branches. These admonitions center on the use of μένω in the passage, and the references to the relationship of the branches to the vine (vv. 4, 5b–7) are stated both positively as a promise and negatively as a warning. The general approach to the passage is allegorical in nature, but does not appear to be created specifically for this use, as an allegory usually is.

The Relation to the Other Discourses

The four metaphorical discourses considered above are all different, but they also demonstrate a common set of patterns. Each particular metaphor is connected to the role of Jesus as the Christ, although the metaphor in chapter 4 is not explicitly connected to an "I am" saying. In chapters 4 and 6, the discourses come without a parabolic statement, although such references are employed in John 10:1–5 (a riddle or dark saying) and in chapter 15 (a near allegory). In all, the evangelist seeks to build his metaphors upon the basis of Old Testament themes, making connections with Jesus as the Christ, who is the primary focus of each metaphor. The author makes identifications so closely that in each case he moves freely between the literal and the figurative. Jesus is thus the center of each of these discourses, as he is throughout the entire Gospel.

---

110. Barrett, *Gospel*, 393.

CONCLUSION

In summary, the use of metaphor is one of the defining characteristics of the author of the Gospel of John. Only in Matthew do we also find a like metaphorical usage, though developed on a much more limited scale. These Johannine metaphors, however, are distinctive because they allow the author the privilege of bringing the strength of his Christian interpretation into his message. The metaphorical union of concepts brings together elements from the ministry of Jesus, viewed through the lens of the evangelist's interpretation, connecting biblical themes and figures within a new synthesis of meaning. The metaphor is then developed to emphasize to the hearer or reader the characteristics or qualities of each element, which become important for the nuances of thought that develop. This development may take the form of a short narration related to the role of the character, a parabolic form, or a short or long discussion of the metaphor itself. In all of these metaphors, there is a concrete union of thought stronger than the simile. Jesus is identified figuratively with the role of the person or object to which he is metaphorically connected, and this union of terminology is one of the rich features of Johannine Christology.

EPILOGUE[1]

Early in the nineteenth century, Connop Thirlwall, a bishop in the Anglican Church, wrote an essay that changed the ways we think about the Gospel of John. Thirlwall showed that the irony found in John's Gospel did not follow the Socratic pattern whereby the conflict was between two people in the narrative, but that it developed in the manner that Sophocles used in writing his tragedies whereby the irony was found between the author of the narrative and his audience.[2] We have noted this fully in the chapter of this work on irony, showing the validity of Thirlwall's approach.

Thus, it should be no surprise that the apostle who wrote the Gospel of John should be acquainted with Greek theater and that he should be influenced by it in his writing of the Fourth Gospel. Rather, we should have expected that this should have happened. Tradition tells us that the apostle John spent a number of years in the area around Ephesus, from which he wrote his Gospel. With this in mind, it is probable that the apostle did become acquainted with the culture of the area and did come in contact with the works of great and popular Greek writers of tragedy. In the early twentieth century, Butler Pratt wrote an article in which he showed the similarity between the structure of the Greek play and the structure of the Gospel.[3] Pratt reconstructed the content of the Gospel, showing that it would fit well into the format used by Aeschylus, Sophocles, or Euripides. While we would not go this far, I do believe that we should look at the basic structure to gain insights into the pattern John used to construct his Gospel. This literary pattern might be added to our list of literary devices.

The three great dramatists of the fifth century BCE were Aeschylus, Sophocles, and Euripides. Each left his mark on the Greek theater. Aeschylus was first, and followed the pattern he received—one actor on stage at

1. This epilogue is a new addition to the revised edition and represents a new line of thinking.

2. Thirlwall, "Irony of Sophocles."

3. Pratt, "Gospel of John," 448–59.

any time—and added a second actor. The openings of his dramas were varied, but usually included a song or a duet that included the chorus. (In most Greek tragedies, music played a significant role.) Sophocles added a third character, and his dramas usually began with a dialogue scene.[4] These dialogues were sometimes between a god or goddess and a human, and at other times between two characters who would play significant roles as the tragedy unfolds.

Euripides was the last of the three. He developed the form even further with the addition of other characters. He also began all of his plays with a prologue. This was a new development in the form that the dramatic tragedies took. This prologue took the form of a monologue and became a key part of the new dramatic form. The speaker was often a god or goddess, but could also be the main character, a secondary character, or even a minor character. A god or goddess spoke the prologue in five of the dramas. These prologues were detached from the action of the drama, and were characterized by the thoroughness with which they provided information to the audience, information that the audience members would need for their understanding of the events that would unfold.[5]

The speeches that formed the prologue were directed to the audience and provided them with necessary information so that they could understand the position of the author and the events of the drama. These prologues have been described as fulfilling the function of the modern "playbill."[6] If a god or goddess spoke, he/she would probably exit the stage and never be seen again as the events unfolded.[7] In this manner, the god seemed to have authority over the events, and his or her absence gave the speaker the approximate role of a narrator. These prologues attempted to let the audience know about the characters (who they were and where they were both in location and in time) as well as what has happened before the drama began.

In all of these dramas, the audience was acquainted with the events of the play before they came to the theater. The characters and events were usually part of the history that had been part of the legends of the nation. The audience came to see how the author would handle the events. Usually, the authors handled the events in a very orthodox manner. However,

---

4. Pratt, "Gospel of John," 449; Vellacott, *Ironic Drama*, 20.

5. Kitto, *Greek Tragedy*, 197.

6. Roberts, "Beginnings and Endings," 138.

7. Roberts, "Beginnings and Endings," 141.

there were occasions where the author—e.g., Euripides's Helen—where the events were portrayed in a significantly different manner than their histories told them.

In Euripides' account of the Trojan War, it is only a phantasm of Helen that is carried off to Troy and causes the war with the Greeks. The real Helen is spirited off to Egypt, where she awaits Orestes to come and liberate her. But in all of the dramas, the prologue speaks with interpretative authority. In the prologue to *Hecuba*, the ghost of Polydores, son of the main character Hecuba, lays out the background of the tragedy, including his own death. Polymestor has been entrusted with a large amount of gold for the boy to have when he comes of age, thus ensuring that Polydores will have a comfortable life. However, Polymestor kills him and claims the gold for his own. But it is not until late in the drama that the body of Polydores washes up on the seashore and that Polymestor, who claims his innocence and lack of knowledge of the death, is convicted of the events. The audience already knows this truth, as it has been revealed to them in the prologue. Thus, even in Euripides, we see the third-person point of view with the events laid out for the audience before the characters in the drama become aware of them.

Following the prologue, Euripides moved directly into the action of the drama. Usually this took the form of a dialogue. Remember, characters on the Greek stage wore heavy masks, and most of the real action occurred off the stage and was reported to the characters (and the audience) by a messenger. Choruses sang their parts as the drama began and continued to its conclusion.

Observe the similarity to the Johannine prologue. In it, John relates the basic facts necessary to properly understand the account that follows. John tells us about the Christ: who he is (the preexistent God), that he assumed humanity when came to earth and carried on a ministry (the apostles beheld his glory through it), and that he fulfilled his mission of revealing his Father to the world. The community of disciples came to faith that Jesus is the Christ through their observance of Jesus' ministry and his teaching. That faith transformed their lives as they became the Sons of God. But not all received him. The account that follows in the Gospel records the individual events, showing the transformations that came about when men accepted Jesus and the conflicts and rejection as witnessed in the lives of others.

The Prologue of John also introduces the other main character, John the Baptist, in the decade before Jesus came on the scene. He is pictured as the first to proclaim Jesus' role as the Messiah and the source of Jesus' first disciples. As with Euripides, John's Gospel moves immediately from the prologue into a series of events, beginning with John and his proclamation that Jesus is the prophesied Lord whose way God sent him to prepare.

In his article in *Biblical World*, Butler Pratt breaks down the Gospel of John into scenes as they would have appeared in a Greek drama.[8] We do not believe that is a profitable exercise, and would not propose following that route. However, we do believe it is profitable to look at the ending of the Greek drama, as Euripides conceived of it, to determine what influence it might have had on John as he composed his Gospel.

The problem that the writers of Greek tragedies faced was common to them all. They needed to bring closure and meaning to events that the audience knew were not the end of the story.[9] They were writing about events that were known to those who came to the theater. The authors could only pick out a significant segment of that history and portray it in the events for the drama. They needed to find a way to bring the drama to an end for the history that did not end. This was especially important because they lived in a time when their audiences apparently struggled with their belief in the gods and the question of their morality as the gods were portrayed in the events of the drama. Euripides has often been accused of sharing in this skepticism. The endings of the play needed to confirm or enable the interpretation of the drama while placing the proper deities in an acceptable light.

There were three methods that Euripides used to bring an end to the drama: *deus ex machina*, an aetiological reference, and the use of a chorus. Often more than one of these elements might be used. Most often, the chorus would come at the very end, and many times the words of the chorus were the same from drama to drama. This final chorus formed a conventional coda.

> Many are the shapes divinities take,
> Much that's unanticipated the gods accomplish,
> What we expect goes unfulfilled,

8. Pratt, "Gospel of John," 456–58.
9. Roberts, "Beginnings and Endings," 142.

And the god finds a way for the unexpected.
Such was the outcome of the matter.[10]

The *deus ex machina* was a device where the god would appear at the end of a drama to bring a word that would bring closure to what had gone on. This action was either accomplished by the use of a crane (μηχανή) or some other device to make it appear that the god was above the action.[11] There were occasions where this was accomplished by placing the god on the roof of a temple. From this lofty position, the god or goddess would speak, revealing a truth that the audience needed to bring meaning and often to interpret the morality of the tragic events they had watched. It was the role of the gods to represent justice in our world.

Many times, the participants in the events were given insight into the divine will, and were thus called to bring their intentions into line with what the gods expected. At the conclusion of *Helen*, when Theoclymenus, king of Egypt, intends to send his entire fleet in pursuit of the small boat that Helen and Menelaus have escaped in as they returned to Greece, the Dioscuri (a pair of gods) intervene, telling Theoclymenus that he must let them proceed, for this is the will of the gods. This word placates his anger, allowing their safe return.

Many of these endings reinforced closure, not only by meeting the expectations raised in the drama, but also "by evoking natural or cultural markers of closure in human lives."[12] They often referred to a ritual or a circumstance that was to take place in the future, but was now a regular part of the culture. The technical term for this device used in endings is the "αἴτιον." For example, in Hippolytus, Artemis declares that, in the future, young Athenian girls will offer up their hair in Hippolytus' honor before their wedding day. These offerings are to commemorate Phaedra's love for Hippolytus, a central cause of his suffering. The regular use of aetiology confirmed the end of the drama. The god's authority was represented in a prophecy that explained an event or institution now a part of life as the prophecy had been fulfilled.

The Greek tragedies needed to bring closure at the end of the drama because the audience knew that the drama was not the end of the action. The audience's memory of the myths of their day would allow the events to continue as the received history continued. This is similar to the problems

10. Roberts, "Beginnings and Endings," 146.

11. Bates, *Euripides*, 27.

12. Roberts, "Beginnings and Endings," 143.

faced by the Gospel writers. Matthew brings his Gospel to a close on the mount of ascension, where the Lord leaves this earth to ascend to the Father. This event brings an end to the resurrection appearances and to Jesus' regular meetings with his disciples. Mark's ending is lost or at least confused, with an ending added to the abrupt ending that most manuscript evidence supports. Luke deals with the problem of closure by writing a sequel to his Gospel. He moved right into the apostolic ministry found in the Book of Acts and the development of the church as a continuation of "all that Jesus began to do and to teach" (Acts 1:1–2). To some extent, two insertions (20:30–31; 21:24–25) seemed to follow the approach taken by the writers of Greek tragedy, with his use of what some have called the epilogue.

While many have looked at the epilogues found at the end of the Gospel of John as evidence of different layers of composition, we find that they are akin to the epilogue as Euripides used it. In John 20:30–31, John ties his purpose for writing the Gospel into the prologue of the Gospel. In the prologue, he declares that he had come to faith through observing the actions of Jesus' ministry, and that this faith had led to the transformation of his life. Through his faith, he had become a child of God, experiencing a spiritual rebirth with God as Father (1:12–13). In this first epilogue, John declares that he has chosen the events recorded in the Gospel specifically so that the readers may experience the teaching of Jesus that led to his rebirth. In a manner similar to his experience of rebirth with God as Father, they also may find their lives enriched by the same experience. The spiritual experience that the apostles had known as they walked with Jesus on a day-to-day basis is available to any who would put faith in Jesus and commit himself/herself to walk with Jesus as the Lord of his/her life. The events chosen to be recorded in this Gospel are sufficient to bring a man or a woman to faith leading to the experience of rebirth.

The second epilogue comes at the very end of the Gospel (21:24–25). This comes after the Resurrection, when Jesus has met with seven disciples on the shore of the Sea of Galilee. Following Jesus' instruction from the shore, they take a miraculous catch of fish. This leads to a series of events on the shore where these seven find themselves face to face with the risen Lord. In the scenes following, Jesus reinstates Peter, commissioning him with the words, "Feed my sheep." This is followed by a prophecy of the martyr death that Peter will die. Peter asks Jesus about the beloved disciple, what manner of death he will die. The text indicates that Jesus' enigmatic words were interpreted by many to mean that he would return before the beloved disciple died. It was this beloved disciple who chose the events to be included in the Gospel and faithfully wrote them down.

Then the second epilogue brings in an outside witness to testify to the authenticity of the events (21:24). This has led many scholars to believe that there is another level of authorship, or at least a second level of editors working on the text. However, if we look at Euripides's techniques involved in his epilogue, we see that this need not be the case. Euripides felt free to bring in an outside god or goddess (*deus ex machina*) or a chorus to bring conclusion to his work. These outside sources were intended to give authority and authenticity to his work. We find this second epilogue in the Gospel of John, using its outside source for this same function. While John does not define for us the "we" who testifies about the truthfulness and choice of the events chosen, he does intend for that source to bring closure to the text and encourages us to accept his choice of events as the right choice of events.

A study of the techniques used by the great Greek authors of the fifth century BCE will not answer all of the issues involved in the study of the literary techniques used in John's Gospel. But they will give us insight into the literary techniques used in the centuries before Christ, upon which the author had to draw. We should ever be reminded that the Biblical writers felt free to use these techniques, e.g., Paul's use of the Asian style of Greek in his composition of Ephesians, taken from the contemporary literary culture. Before the time of the printing press, the dramatic stage played a much greater role in the literary scene than the printed page does today.

BIBLIOGRAPHY

Akala, Adesola Joan. *The Son-Father Relationship and Christological Symbolism in the Gospel of John.* LNTS 505. London: Bloomsbury, 2014.

Anderson, Paul N. *The Christology of the Fourth Gospel: Its Unity and Disunity in the Light of John 6.* WUNT 2.78. Tübingen, Germany: Mohr Siebeck, 1996.

———. "Gradations of Symbolization in the Johannine Passion Narrative: Control Measures for Theologizing Speculation Gone Awry." In *Imagery in the Gospel of John: Terms, Forms, Themes, and Theology of Johannine Figurative Language,* edited by Jörg Frey et al., 157–94. WUNT 200. Tübingen, Germany: Mohr Siebeck, 2006.

Aristotle. *The Poetics.* Translated by W. H. Fyfe. London: Harvard University Press, 1932.

Ball, David Mark. *'I Am' in John's Gospel: Literary Function, Background and Theological Implications.* JSNTSS 124. Sheffield: Sheffield Academic Press, 1996.

Barrett, C. K. *The Gospel According to St. John.* London: SPCK, 1955.

———. "The Lamb of God." *NTS* 1 (1953–1954) 210–19.

———. "The Old Testament in the Fourth Gospel." *JTS* 48 (1947) 155–69.

Bates, William N. *Euripides: A Student of Human Nature.* Philadelphia: University of Pennsylvania Press, 1930.

Bauer, Walter. *Das Johannesevangelium.* HNT 6. Tübingen, Germany: Mohr Siebeck, 1925.

———. *A Greek-English Lexicon of the New Testament.* Translated by W. Arndt and F. W. Gingrich. Chicago: University of Chicago Press, 1957.

Belle, Gilbert van. *Les Parentheses dans l'Évangile de Jean.* Leuven, Belgium: Leuven University Press, 1985.

———. *The Signs Source in the Fourth Gospel.* BETL 116. Leuven, Belgium: Leuven University Press, 1994.

Bernard, John H. *A Critical and Exegetical Commentary on the Gospel According to St. John.* 2 vols. ICC. Edinburgh, UK: T. & T. Clark, 1928.

Beutler, Johannes, and Robert T. Fortna, eds. *The Shepherd Discourse of John 10 and Its Context: Studies by Members of the Johannine Writings Seminar.* SNTSMS 67. Cambridge: Cambridge University Press, 1991.

Bishop, E. F. F. "The Door of the Sheep: John 10:7–9." *ExpT* 71 (1960) 307–9.

Blank, Josef. "Der Verhandlung vor Pilatus: John 18:28—19:16, im Lichte Johanneischer Theologie." *BZ* 3 (1959) 60–81.

Blass, F., et al. *A Greek Grammar of the New Testament and Other Early Christian Literature.* Chicago: University of Chicago Press, 1961.

Boers, Hendrikus. *Neither on This Mountain Not in Jerusalem: A Study of John 4.* SBLMS 35. Atlanta: Scholars, 1988.

Booth, Wayne C. *The Rhetoric of Fiction.* Chicago: University of Chicago Press, 1963.

Borgen, Peder. *Bread from Heaven.* NovTSup 6. Leiden, Netherlands: Brill, 1965.

Botha, J. E. "The Case of Johannine Irony Reopened I: The Problematic Current Situation." *Neotestamentica* 25 (1991) 209–20.

———. "The Case of Johannine Irony Reopened II: Suggestions, Alternative Approaches." *Neotestamentica* 25 (1991) 221–32.

Brant, Jo-Ann. *Dialogue and Drama: Elements of Greek Tragedy in the Fourth Gospel.* Peabody, MA: Hendrickson, 2004.

Brooks, Cleanth. "Irony as a Principle of Structure." *Literary Opinion in America* 2 (1951) 729–41.

Brown, Francis, et al. *A Hebrew and English Lexicon of the Old Testament with an Appendix Containing the Biblical Aramaic.* Oxford: Clarendon, 1959.

Brown, Raymond E. *The Gospel According to John (i–xii).* AB 29 and 29A. Garden City, NY: Doubleday, 1966.

———. *The Gospel According to John (xiii–xxi).* AB 29A. Garden City, NY: Doubleday, 1970.

———. "The Kerygma of the Gospel According to John." *Int* 21 (1967) 387–400.

Brown, Stephen J. *The World of Imagery.* London: Paul, 1927.

Bruns, J. Edgar. "The Use of Time in the Fourth Gospel." *NTS* 13 (1966–1967) 285–90.

Büchsel, Friedrich. *Das Evangelium nach Johannes.* NTD 4. Göttingen: Vandenhoeck & Ruprecht, 1949.

Bultmann, Rudolf. *Das Evangelium des Johannes.* KEK. Göttingen: Vandenhoeck & Ruprecht, 1941.

———. *Die Geschichte der Synoptischen Tradition.* 7th ed. Göttingen: Vandenhoeck & Ruprecht, 1967.

———. "Johannesevangelium." *RGG*3 3:843.

———. *The Gospel of John, A Commentary.* Translated by G. R. Beasley-Murray et al. Philadelphia: Westminster Press, 1971.

———. *Theologie des Neuen Testaments.* Tübingen, Germany: Mohr Siebeck, 1958.

Burney, Charles F. *The Aramaic Origin of the Fourth Gospel.* Oxford: Clarendon Press, 1922.

Busse, Ulrich. *Das Johannesevanglium: Bildlichkeit, Diskurs und Ritual.* BETL 162. Leuven, Belgium: Leuven University Press, 2002.

Carr, A. "A Note on St. John 7:52: A Prophet or the Prophet?" *Expositor* 8 (1903) 219–26.

Carson, Donald. *The Gospel According to John.* Grand Rapids: Eerdmans, 1991.

Carson, D. A. "Understanding Misunderstandings in the Fourth Gospel." *Tyndale Bulletin* 33 (1982) 59–91.

Cerfaux, Lucien. "Le Thème Litteraire Parabolique dans L'évangile de Saint Jean." ConBNT 11 (1947) 15–25.

Chanikuzhy, Jacob. *Jesus, the Eschatological Temple: An Exegetical Study of Jn 2.13–22 in the Light of the Pre 70 C.E. Eschatological Temple Hopes and the Synoptic Temple Action.* Contributions to Biblical Exegesis & Theology 58. Leuven, Belgium: Peeters, 2012.

Charlier, J. P. "La Notion de Signe (σημεῖον) dans le IV Évangile." *RSPT* 43 (1959) 434–48.

Chatman, Seymour. *Story and Discourse: Narrative Structure in Fiction and Film.* Ithaca, NY: Cornell University Press, 1978.

Clavier, Henri. "L'Ironie dans le Quatrième Évangile." In *SE 1*, edited by K. Aland, 261–76. TU 73. Berlin: Akademie, 1959.

Cohen, Simon. "The Political Background of the Words of Amos." *HUCA* 36 (1965) 153–60.

Coloe, Mary L. *Dwelling in the Household of God: Johannine Ecclesiology and Spirituality.* Collegeville, PA: Liturgical, 2007.

———. *God Dwells with Us: Temple Symbolism in the Fourth Gospel.* Collegeville, PA: Liturgical, 2001.

Colson, F. H., and G. Whitaker, eds. *Philo.* LCL. 10 vols. London: Heinemann, 1929–1953.

Connolly, Francis X. *A Rhetoric Case Book.* New York: Harcourt, 1953.

Cornford, Francis M. *The Origin of Attic Comedy.* Cambridge: Cambridge University Press, 1934.

Counet, Patrick Chatelion. *John, a Postmodern Gospel: Introduction to Deconstructive Exegesis Applied to the Fourth Gospel.* BINS 44. Leiden, Netherlands: Brill, 2000.

Crossan, John Dominic. *In Fragments: The Aphorisms of Jesus.* San Francisco: Harper & Row, 1983.

Cullmann, Oscar. "Der Johanneische Gebrauch Doppeldeutiger Ausdrücke als Schlüssel zum Verständis des Vierten Evangeliums." *TZ* 4 (1948) 360–72.

———. *Die Christologie des Neuen Testaments.* Tübingen, Germany: Mohr Siebeck, 1957.

———. *Heil als Geschichte.* Tübingen, Germany: Mohr Siebeck, 1965.

———. "L'Évangile Johannique et l'Histoire du Salut." *NTS* 11 (1964–1965) 111–22.

———. *Urchristentum und Gottesdienst.* Zurich: Zwingli, 1962.

Culpepper, R. Alan. *Anatomy of the Fourth Gospel: A Study in Literary Design.* Philadelphia: Fortress, 1983.

———. "C. H. Dodd as a Precursor to Narrative Criticism." In *Engaging with C. H. Dodd on the Gospel of John: Sixty Years of Tradition and Interpretation,* edited by Tom Thatcher and Catrin H. Williams, 31–48. Cambridge: Cambridge University Press, 2013.

———. "Cognition in John: The Johannine Signs as Recognition Scenes." *Perspectives in Religious Studies* 35 (2008) 251–60.

———. *Critical Readings of John 6.* BINS 22. Leiden, Netherlands: Brill, 1997.

———. "Designs for the Church in the Gospel Accounts of Jesus' Death." *NTS* 51 (2005) 376–92.

———. "Reading Johannine Irony." In *Exploring the Gospel of John,* edited by R. Alan Culpepper and C. Clifton Black, 193–207. Louisville: Knox, 1996.

———. "Symbolism and History in John's Account of Jesus' Death." In *Anatomies of Narrative Criticism: The Past, Present, and Futures of the Fourth Gospel as Literature,* edited by Tom Thatcher and Stephen D. Moore, 39–54. SBL Resources for Biblical Study 55. Atlanta: Society of Biblical Literature, 2008.

———. "The Theology of the Johannine Passion Narrative: John 19:16b–30." *Neotestamentica* 31 (1997) 21–37.

Dahl, Nils A. "Anamnesis: Mémoire et Commémoration dans le Christianisme Primitive." *ST* 1 (1947) 69–95.

———. "The Parables of Growth." *ST* 5 (1951) 133–66.

———. "Gleichnis und Parabel." In *RGG3* 2:1619.

Day, Janeth Norfleete. *The Woman at the Well: Interpretation of John 4:1–42 in Retrospect and Prospect.* BINS 61. Leiden, Netherlands: Brill, 2002.

de Boer, Martin C. "Narrative Criticism, Historical Criticism and the Gospel of John." *JSNT* 47 (1992) 35–48.

Deissmann, Adolf. *Neue Bibelstudien.* Marburg: Verlagsbuchhandlung, 1895.

Dibelius, Martin. *Die Formgeschichte des Evangeliums.* 5th ed. Tübingen, Germany: Mohr Siebeck, 1966.

Dodd, C. H. *Interpretation of the Fourth Gospel*. Cambridge: Cambridge University Press, 1953.

———. *Historical Tradition in the Fourth Gospel*. Cambridge: Cambridge University Press, 1963.

———. "Une Parabole Cachée dans le Quatrième Évangile." *RHPR* 42 (1962) 107–15.

Doty, William G. *Contemporary New Testament Interpretation*. Englewood Cliffs, NJ: Prentice-Hall, 1972.

Duke, Paul D. *Irony in the Fourth Gospel*. Atlanta: Knox, 1985.

Emery, H. G., and K. G. Brewster, eds. *The New Century Dictionary of the English Language*. 2 vols. New York: Appleton, 1946.

Feuillet, André. "Les ἐγὼ εἰμί Christologiques du Quatrième Évangile." *RSR* 54 (1966) 5–22, 213–40.

Formesyn, Roland. "Le Sèmeion Johannique et le Sèmeion Hellenistique." *Ephemerides Theologicae Lovanienses* 38 (1962) 856–94.

Fortna, Robert T. *The Fourth Gospel and Its Predecessor: From Narrative Source to Present Gospel*. Philadelphia: Fortress, 1988.

———. *The Gospel of Signs: A Reconstruction of the Narrative Source Underlying the Fourth Gospel*. SNTMS 11. Cambridge: Cambridge University Press, 1970.

Freed, Edwin D. "Variations in Language and Thought of John." *ZNW* 55 (1964) 167–97.

Frye, Northrop. *Anatomy of Criticism*. Princeton: Princeton University Press, 1957.

Galling, Kurt, ed. *Die Religion in Geschichte und Gegenwart*. 6 vols. Tübingen, Germany: Mohr Siebeck, 1957–1962.

Gardner-Smith, Percival. *Saint John and the Synoptic Gospels*. Cambridge: Cambridge University Press, 1938.

Genette, Gérard. *Narrative Discourse: An Essay in Method*. Translated by Jane E. Lewin. Ithaca, NY: Cornell University Press, 1980.

Gingrich, F. W. "Ambiguity of Word Meaning in John's Gospel." *Classical Weekly* 37 (1943) 77.

Godet, Frederic L. *Kommentar zu dem Evangelium des Johannes*. Translated by E. Reineck and L. Schmid. Hannover, Germany: Meyer, 1903.

Good, Edwin M. *Irony in the Old Testament*. London: Westminster, 1965.

Gregory, Justina. *A Companion to Greek Tragedy*. Malden, MA: Wiley-Blackwell, 2005.

Gundry, Robert H. "In My Father's House are Many *Monai* (John 14:2)." *ZNW* 58 (1967) 68–72.

Haenchen, Ernst. "Das Johannesevangelium und sein Kommentar." *TLZ* 89 (1964) 881–98.

———. "Der Vater der Mich Gesandt Hat." *NTS* 9 (1962/63) 214.

———. "Jesus vor Pilatus (Joh. 18:28—19:15)." *TLZ* 85 (1960) 93–102.

Harnack, Adolf von. *Bruchstücke des Evangeliums und der Apolcalypse des Petrus*. Leipzig, Germany: Hinrichs, 1893.

———. "Das 'Wir' in den Johanneischen Schriften." *SPAW* 17 (1923) 96–113.

Harner, P. B. *The "I Am" of the Fourth Gospel*. Philadelphia: Fortress, 1970.

Harvey, William J. *The Art of George Eliot*. London: Oxford University Press, 1969.

Hatch, Edwin. *Essays in Biblical Greek*. Oxford: Clarendon, 1889.

Hauck, Frederick. "παροιμία." In *TWNT* 5:854.

Haury, Auguste. *L'Ironie et l'Humour chez Cicéron*. Leiden, Netherlands: Brill, 1955.

Hofbeck, Sebald. *Semeion: Der Begriff des Zeichens im Johannesevangelium unter Berücksichtigung seiner Vorgeschichte.* Münsterschwarzach, Germany: Vier-Turme, 1966.

Hooke, S. H. *Alpha and Omega: A Study in the Pattern of Revelation.* London: Nisbet, 1961.

Hoskyns, Edwin C. *The Fourth Gospel.* Edited by Francis N. Davey. London: Faber & Faber, 1947.

Hunter, Archibald M. *The Gospel According to John.* CBC. Cambridge: Cambridge University Press, 1965.

Jankélévitch, Vladimir. *L'Ironie.* Paris: Alcan, 1936.

Jeremias, Joachim. "ἀμνὸς τοῦ θεοῦ—παῖς θεοῦ." *ZNW* 34 (1935) 115–28.

————. "Μωϋσῆς." In *TWNT* 4:867.

————. "ποιμήν." In *TWNT* 6:494.

————. *The Rediscovery of Bethesda.* Louisville: Southern Baptist Theological Seminary, 1966.

Jones, Larry Paul. *The Symbol of Water in the Gospel of John.* JSNTSS 145. Sheffield: Sheffield Academic Press, 1997.

Jónsson, Jakob. *Humor and Irony in the New Testament.* Copenhagen: Menningarsjols, 1965.

Jülicher, Adolf. *Die Gleichnisreden Jesu.* Tübingen, Germany: Mohr Siebeck, 1910.

Kähler, Martin. *The So-Called Historical Jesus and the Historic Biblical Christ.* Edited and translated by Carl E. Braaten. Philadelphia: Fortress, 1964.

Käsemann, Ernst. *Exegetische Versuche und Besinnungen.* Vol. 1. Göttingen, Germany: Vandenhoeck & Ruprecht, 1960.

Keck, Leander E. "Will the Historical-Critical Method Survive? Some Observations." In *Orientation by Disorientation: Studies in Literary Criticism, Presented in Honor of William A. Beardslee,* edited by Richard A. Spencer, 115–27. Pittsburgh Theological Monograph Series 35. Pittsburgh: Pickwick, 1980.

Keller, Carl-Albert. *Das Wort 'Oth als Offebarungszeichen Gottes.* Basel, Germany: Hoenen, 1946.

Kerr, Alan R. *The Temple of Jesus' Body: The Temple Theme in the Gospel of John.* JSNTSS 220. Sheffield: Sheffield Academic Press, 2002.

Kiefer, Odo. *Die Hirtenrede.* SBS 23. Stuttgart, Germany: Bibelwerk, 1967.

Kim, Jean K. *Woman and Nation: An Intercontextual Reading of the Gospel of John from a Postcolonial Feminist Perspective.* BINS 69. Leiden, Netherlands: Brill, 2004.

Kittel, Gerhard. "*iad`qeph* = ὑψωθῆναι = gekreuzigt warden." *ZNW* 35 (1936) 282–85.

Kittel, Gerhard, and Gerhard Friedrich, eds. *TWNT.* 9 vols. Stuttgart, Germany: Kohlhammer, 1933–1973.

Kitto, Humphrey D. F. *Greek Tragedy: A Literary Study.* New York: Doubleday, 1954.

Koester, Craig R. *Symbolism in the Fourth Gospel: Meaning, Mystery, and Community.* Second edition. Minneapolis: Fortress, 2003.

Koester, Helmut. *Ancient Christian Gospels: Their History and Development.* Philadelphia: Trinity, 1990.

Konrad, Hedwig. *Étude sur la Métaphore.* Paris: Vrin, 1919.

Kysar, Robert. *The Fourth Evangelist and His Gospel: An Examination of Contemporary Scholarship.* Minneapolis: Augsburg, 1975.

————. "Johannine Metaphor—Meaning and Function: A Literary Case Study of John 10:1–18." *Semeia* 53 (1991) 81–111.

La Potterie, Ignace de. "Jésus Roi et Juge d'Après Jo. 19:13: ἐκάθισεν ἐπὶ βήματος." *Bib* 41 (1960) 217–47.

Lampe, Geoffrey W. H., and Kenneth J. Woollcombe. *Essays on Typology*. SBT 22. London: SCM, 1957.

Larsen, Kasper Bro. *Recognizing the Stranger: Recognition Scenes in the Gospel of John*. BINS 93. Leiden, Netherlands: Brill, 2008.

Lee, Dorothy A. *The Symbolic Narratives of the Fourth Gospel: The Interplay of Form and Meaning*. JSNTSS 95. Sheffield: Sheffield Academic Press, 1994.

Léon-Dufour, Xavier. "Towards a Symbolic Reading of the Fourth Gospel." *NTS* 27 (1981) 439–56.

———. "Trois Chiasmes Johanniques." *NTS* 7 (1960–1961) 249–55.

Leroy, Herbert. *Rätsel und Missverständnis: Ein Beitrag zur Formgeschichte des Johannesevangeliums*. Bonner Biblische Beiträge 30. Bonn, Germany: Peter Hanstein, 1968.

Lightfoot, Robert H. *St. John's Gospel: A Commentary*. Edited by C. F. Evans. Oxford: Clarendon Press, 1957.

Lindars, Barnabas. *New Testament Apologetics: The Doctrinal Significance of the Old Testament*. London: SCM, 1961.

Lohmeyer, Ernst. *Das Evangelium des Matthäus*. Edited by Werner Schmauch. KEK. Göttingen, Germany: Vandenhoeck & Ruprecht, 1962.

Lonergan, Bernard. *De Verbo Incarnato*. Rome: Gregorian University Press, 1964.

Lubbock, Percy. *The Craft of Fiction*. London: Cape, 1926.

Lund, N. W. "The Influence of Chiasmus upon the Structure of the Gospels." *Anglican Theological Review* 13 (1931) 27–48, 405–33.

Maccini, Robert Gordon. *Her Testimony is True: Women as Witnesses according to John*. JSNTS 125. Sheffield, UK: Sheffield Academic Press, 1995.

MacRae, George W. "Theology and Irony in the Fourth Gospel." In *The Word in the World: Essays in Honor of Frederick L. Moriarity, S.J.*, edited by Richard J. Clifford and George W. MacRae, 83–96. Cambridge: Weston College Press, 1973.

Martyn, J. Louis. *History and Theology in the Fourth Gospel*. New York: Harper & Row, 1968.

McCool, Francis. *Introduction in Novum Testamentum: Problemata Johannaea*. Rome: Pontificium Institutum Biblicum, 1965.

Meeks, Wayne A. *The Prophet King: Moses Traditions and the Johannine Christology*. NovTSup 14. Leiden, Germany: Brill, 1967.

Menoud, Philippe-H. "Le Fils de Joseph." *RTP* 18 (1930) 275–88.

Metzger, Bruce M. *The Text of the New Testament: Its Transmission, Corruption, and Transmission*. New York: Oxford University Press, 1964.

Michel. "Mimhskomai." In *TWNT* 4:676–81.

Mollat, Donatien. "Le Sèmeion Johannique." *Sacra Pagina* 2 (1959) 209–18.

Mollat, Donatien, and F. M. Braun. *L'Évangile et les Épitres de Saint Jean*. Le Sainte Bible. Paris: Cerf, 1960.

Moloney, Francis J. "The Function of John 13–17 within the Johannine Narrative." In *Literary and Social Readings of the Fourth Gospel*, edited by Fernando F. Segovia, 43–66. Vol. 2 of *What Is John?*; SympS 7. Atlanta: Scholars, 1998.

Moore, Stephen D. "Are There Impurities in the Living Water that the Johannine Jesus Dispenses? Deconstruction, Feminism, and the Samaritan Woman." In

Poststructuralism and the New Testament: Derrida and Foucault at the Foot of the Cross, 43–64. Minneapolis: Fortress, 1994.

———. *Literary Criticism and the Gospels: The Theoretical Challenge*. New Haven: Yale University Press, 1989.

Moulton, James H. *A Grammar of the New Testament Greek, Volume 1: Prolegomena*. Edinburgh, UK: T. & T. Clark, 1908.

Moulton, James H., and George Milligan. *The Vocabulary of the Greek New Testament*. London: Hodder and Stoughton, 1959.

Müller, Theophil E. *Das Heilsgeschehen im Johannesevangelium*. Zurich: Gotthelf, 1961.

Mussner, Franz. *The Historical Jesus in the Gospel of St. John*. New York: Herder & Herder, 1967.

Ng, W. *Water Symbolism in John: An Eschatological Interpretation*. New York: Lang, 2001.

Noack, Bent. *Zur Johanneischen Tradition*. Copenhagen, Denmark: Rosenkilde and Bagger, 1954.

O'Day, Gail R. *Revelation in the Fourth Gospel: Narrative Mode and Theological Claim*. Philadelphia: Fortress, 1986.

Paschal, R. Wade, Jr. "Sacramental Symbolism and Physical Imagery in the Gospel of John." *Tyndale Bulletin* 32 (1981) 151–76.

Painter, John. "Johannine Symbols: A Case Study in Epistemology." *Journal of Theology for Southern Africa* 27 (1979) 26–41.

Peterson, Norman R. *Literary Criticism for New Testament Critics*. Guides to Biblical Scholarship. Philadelphia: Fortress, 1978.

———. "Literary Criticism in Biblical Studies." In *Orientation by Disorientation: Studies in Literary Criticism, Presented in Honor of William A. Beardslee*, edited by Richard A. Spencer, 25–50. Pittsburgh Theological Monograph Series 35. Pittsburgh: Pickwick, 1980.

Plato. *Euthyphro, Apology, Crito, Phaedo, Phaedrus*. Translated by Harold N. Fowler. LCL. London: Heinemann, 1933.

Porter, Stanley E. *John, His Gospel, and Jesus: In Pursuit of the Johannine Voice*. Grand Rapids: Eerdmans, 2015.

Powell, Mark Allan. *What Is Narrative Criticism?* Guides to Biblical Scholarship. Minneapolis: Fortress, 1990.

Pratt, D. Butler. "The Gospel of John from the Standpoint of Greek Tragedy." *Biblical World* 30 (1907) 448–59.

Reicke, Bo. *Diakonie, Festfreude und Zelos in Verbindung mit der Altchristlichen Agapenfeier*. Uppsala, Sweden: Lundequist, 1951.

Reicke, Bo, and L. Rost, eds. *Biblisch-historisches Handwörterbuch*. 4 vols. Gottingen: Vandenhoeck & Ruprecht, 1962.

Rengstorf, Karl Heinrich. "σημεῖον…" In *The Theological Dictionary of the New Testament*, edited by Gerhard Kittel and Gerhard Friedrich, translated by Geoffrey W. Bromiley, 7:201–61. Grand Rapids: Eerdmans, 1971.

Resseguie, James L. *The Strange Gospel: Narrative Design and Point of View in John*. BINS 56. Leiden, Netherlands: Brill, 2001.

Richard, E. "Expressions of Double Meaning and Their Function in the Gospel of John." *NTS* 31 (1985) 96–112.

Roberts, Deborah H. "Beginnings and Endings." In *A Companion to Greek Tragedy*, edited by Justina Gregory, 136–48. Malden, MA: Blackwell, 2005.

Robinson, John A. T. "The Parable of the Good Shepherd (John 10:1–5)." *ZNW* 46 (1955) 233–40.

Ruckstuhl, Eugen. *Die Literarische Einheit des Johannesevangeliums: Der Gegenwärtige Stand des Einschlägigen Erforschung*. Studia Friburgensia 3. Freiburg, Switzerland: Paulus-Verlag, 1951.

Salmon, George. *A Historical Introduction to the Study of the Books of the New Testament*. London: Murray, 1889.

Schlatter, Adolf. *Der Evangelist Johannes, ein Kommentar zum Vierten Evangelium*. Stuttgart, Germany: Calwer, 1960.

Schlier, Heinrich. "Jesus und Pilatus—nach dem Johannesevangelium." In *Die Zeit der Kirche*, 57–60. Freiburg, Germany: Herder & Herder, 1956.

Schmidt, Karl L. "Der Johannesiche Charakter der Erzählung vom Hochzeitwunder in Kana." In *Harnack Ehrung*, 32–43. Leipzig, Germany: Hinrichs, 1921.

Schnackenburg, Rudolf. *Das Johannesevangelium*. Vol. 1. HThKNT 4. Freiburg, Germany: Herder & Herder, 1965.

———. "Die Erwartung des 'Propheten' nach dem Neuen Testament und den Qumran-Texten." Pages 622–39 in *SE*. Edited by Kurt Aland. Berlin: Akademie Verlag, 1959.

———. *The Gospel According to St. John*. Vol. 1. Translated by Kevin Smyth. HTCNT. New York: Herder & Herder, 1968.

Schneiders, Sandra M. "History and Symbolism in the Fourth Gospel." In *L'Evangile de Jean: Sources, Redaction, Théologie*, edited by Marinus de Jonge, 371–76. Bibliotheca Ephemeridum Theologicarum Lovaniensium 44. Gembloux, Belgium: Duculot, 1977.

———. "The Raising of the New Temple: John 20.19–23 and Johannine Ecclesiology." *NTS* 52 (2006) 337–55.

———. "Symbolism and the Sacramental Principle in the Fourth Gospel." In *Segni e Sacramenti nel Vangelo di Giovanni*, edited by Pius-Ramon Tragan, 221–35. Studia Anselmiana 66. Rome: Anselmiana, 1977.

Schulz, Siegfried. *Komposition und Herkunft der Johanneischen Reden*. Stuttgart, Germany: Kohlhammer, 1960.

Schwankl, Otto. *Licht und Finsternis: Ein Metaphorisches Paradigma in den Johanneischen Schriften*. HBS 5. Freiburg, Germany: Herder, 1995.

Schweizer, Eduard. *Ego Eimi: Die Religionsgeshichtliche Herkunft und Theologische Bedeutung der Johanneischen Bildreden, zugleich ein Beitrag zur Quellenfrage des vierten Evangeliums*. FRLANT 38. Göttingen, Germany: Vandenhoeck & Ruprecht, 1939.

Sedgewick, Garnett G. *Of Irony, Especially in Drama*. Toronto: University of Toronto Press, 1935.

Smith, Dwight Moody, Jr. "Book Review: The Literary Devices in John's Gospel." *Interpretation* 26.1 (1972) 119–20.

———. *Composition and Order of the Fourth Gospel: Bultmann's Literary Theory*. The Johannine Monograph Series 2. Eugene, OR: Wipf & Stock, 2015.

Spitta, Friedrich. "Die Hirtengleichnisse des Vierten Evangeliums." *ZNW* 10 (1909) 59–80, 103–27.

Stählin, Wilhelm. *Zur Psychologie und Statistik der Metapher*. Leipzig: Engelmann, 1913.

Staley, Jeffrey Loyd. *The Print's First Kiss: A Rhetorical Investigation of the Implied Reader in the Fourth Gospel*. SBLDS 82. Atlanta: Scholars, 1988.

Stanford, William B. *Greek Metaphor: Studies in Theory and Practice.* Oxford: Blackwell, 1936.

Stemberger, Günter. *La Symbolique du Bien et du Mal selon Saint Jean.* Parole de Dieu. Paris: Editions du Seuil, 1970.

Stendahl, Krister. *The School of St. Matthew.* Uppsala, Sweden: Gleerup, 1954.

Stern, Gustaf. *Meaning and Change of Meaning.* Bloomington: Indiana University Press, 1932.

Strack, Hermann L., and Paul Billerbeck. "Dreisigster Exkurs: Vorzeichen und Berechnung der Tage des Messias." In *Kommentar zum Neuen Testament aus Talmud und Midrasch,* 4.997–1015. Munich: Beck, 1922–1926.

Strathmann, Hermann. *Das Evangelium nach Johannes.* NTD 4. Göttingen: Vandenhoeck & Ruprecht, 1963.

Tasker, R. V. G. *The Gospel According to St. John.* TNTC. London: Tyndale, 1960.

Tenney, M. C. "The Footnotes of John's Gospel." *Bibliotheca Sacra* 117 (1960) 350–64.

Thatcher, Tom, and Stephen D. Moore, eds. *Anatomies of Narrative Criticism: The Past, Present, and Futures of the Fourth Gospel as Literature.* Atlanta: Society of Biblical Literature, 2008.

Thirlwall, Connop. "On the Irony of Sophocles." In *Essays, Speeches, Sermons, etc.,* edited by J. J. S. Perowne, 143–48. Remains Literary and Theological 3. London: Daidy, 1878.

Thomaskutty, Johnson. *Dialogue in the Book of Signs: A Polyvalent Analysis of John 1:19–12:50.* BINS 136. Leiden, Netherlands: Brill, 2015.

Thompson, Alan R. *The Dry Mock: A Study of Irony in Drama.* Berkeley: University of California Press, 1948.

Thomson, James A. K. *Irony: An Historical Introduction.* Cambridge, MA: Harvard University Press, 1926.

Thyen, Hartwig. "Aus der Literatur zum Johannesevangelium." *Theologische Rundschau* 39 (1974) 43.

Toelken, J. B. "An Oral Canon for the Child Ballads: Construction and Application." *Journal of the Folklore Institute* 4 (1967) 75–102.

Tolmie, D. Francois. *Jesus' Farewell to the Disciples: John 13:1–17:26 in Narratological Perspective.* BINS 12. Leiden, Netherlands: Brill, 1995.

Torm, Frederick. *Hermeneutik des Neuen Testaments.* Göttingen, Germany: Vandenhoeck & Ruprecht, 1930.

Um, Stephen T. *The Theme of Temple Christology in John's Gospel.* LNTS 312. London: T. & T. Clark, 2006.

Uspensky, Boris. *A Poetics of Composition: The Structure of the Artistic Text and Typology of a Compositional Form.* Translated by V. Zavarin and S. Wittig. Berkeley: University of California Press, 1973.

van der Watt, Jan G. "Ethics Alive in Imagery." In *Imagery in the Gospel of John: Terms, Forms, Themes, and Theology of Johannine Figurative Language,* edited by Jörg Frey et al., 421–48. WUNT 200. Tübingen, Germany: Mohr Siebeck, 2006.

———. *Family of the King: Dynamics of Metaphor in the Gospel according to John.* BINS 47. Leiden, Netherlands: Brill, 2000.

———. "Interpreting Imagery in John's Gospel: John 10 and 15 as Case Studies." In *Hypomnema: Feesbundel opgedra aan Prof J P Louw,* edited by J. H. Barkhuizen et al., 272–82. Pretoria, South Africa: University of Pretoria, 1992.

———. "'Metaphorik' in Joh 15,1–8." *BZ* 38 (1994) 67–80.

————. "Symbolism in John's Gospel: An Evaluation of Dodd's Contribution." In *Engaging with C. H. Dodd on the Gospel of John: Sixty Years of Tradition and Interpretation*, edited by Tom Thatcher and Catrin H. Williams, 66–85. Cambridge: Cambridge University Press, 2013.

Vellacott, Phillip. *Ironic Drama: A Study of Euripides' Method and Meaning*. Cambridge: Cambridge University Press, 1975.

Vergote, Antoine. "L'Exaltation du Christ en Croix selon le Quatrième Évangile." *ETL* 28 (1952) 10–23.

von Harnack, Adolf. "Das 'Wir' in den Johanneischen Scriften." Report of a meeting of the Prussian Academy of Sciences. Berlin: Preussischen Akademie der Wissenschaften. 1923.

Von Wahlde, Urban C. *The Gospel and Letters of John*. 3 vols. Eerdmans Critical Commentary. Grand Rapids: Eerdmans, 2010.

Wead, David W. "The Johannine Double Meaning." *Restoration Quarterly* 13 (1970) 106–20.

————. "Johannine Irony as a Key to the Author-Audience Relationship in John's Gospel." In *American Academy of Religion: Biblical Literature, 1974*, compiled by Fred O. Francis, 33–50. Tallahassee: American Academy of Religion, 1974.

————. "We Have a Law." *Novum Testamentum* 11 (1969) 185–89.

Westcott, Brooke F. *The Gospel According to St. John*. London: John Murray, 1919.

Wikenhauser, Alfred. *Das Evangelium nach Johannes*. Regensburg, Germany: Pustet, 1948.

Wiles, Maurice F. *The Spiritual Gospel: The Interpretation of the Fourth Gospel in the Early Church*. Cambridge: Cambridge University Press, 1960.

Williams, Catrin H. *I Am He: The Meaning and Interpretation of 'Anî Hû' in Jewish and Early Christian Literature*. WUNT 2:113. Tübingen, Germany: Mohr Siebeck, 2000.

Winter, Paul. *On the Trial of Jesus*. SJ 1. Berlin: Gruyter, 1961.

Woude, A. S. van der. *Die Messianischen Vorstellungen der Gemeinde von Qumran*. SSN 3. Assen, Netherlands: Gorcum, 1957.

Zahn, Theodor. *Das Evangelium des Johannes*. Komnmentar zum Neuen Testament 4. Leipzig, Germany: Deichert, 1908.

Ziener, Georg. "Weisheitsbuch und Johannesevangelium." *Bib* 38 (1957) 396–418.

Zimmermann, Ruben. *Christologie der Bilder im Johannesevangelium: Die Christopoetik des vierten Evangeliums unter besonderer Berücksichtigung von Joh 10*. WUNT 171. Tübingen, Germany: Siebeck, 2004.

————. "Metapherntheorie und Biblische Bildersprache: Ein Methodologischer Versuch." *TZ* 56 (2000) 108–33.

————. "Opening Up Paths into the Tangled Thicket of John's Figurative World." In *The Gospel of John: Terms, Forms, Themes and Theology of Figurative Language*, edited by Jörg Frey et al., 1–43. WUNT 200. Tübingen, Germany: Mohr Siebeck, 2006.

————. "Paradigmen einer Metaphorischen Christologie: Eine Leseanleitung." In *Metaphorik und Christologie*, edited by Jörg Frey, Jan Rohls, and Ruben Zimmermann, 1–34. TBT 120. Berlin: Gruyter, 2003.

Zumstein, Jean. "Johannes 19, 25–27." In *Kreative Erinnerung: Relecture und Auslegung im Johannesevangelium*, 156–77. Second edition. ATANT 84. Zürich, Switzerland: Verlag, 2004.